31143011500932
378.001 Craig, R
Craig, Ryan,
College disrupted :

Main

D0437015

COLLEGE
DISRUPTED

COLLEGE
DISRUPTED

THE GREAT UNBUNDLING OF HIGHER EDUCATION

RYAN CRAIG

palgrave
macmillan

COLLEGE DISRUPTED: THE GREAT UNBUNDLING OF HIGHER
EDUCATION
Copyright © Ryan Craig, 2015.
All rights reserved.

First published in 2015 by PALGRAVE MACMILLAN® TRADE in the
United States–a division of St. Martin's Press LLC, 175 Fifth Avenue, New
York, NY 10010.

Palgrave® and Macmillan® are registered trademarks in the United States,
the United Kingdom, Europe and other countries.

ISBN: 978-1-137-27969-9

Library of Congress Cataloging-in-Publication Data

Craig, Ryan, 1972–
    College disrupted : the great unbundling of higher education / Ryan Craig.
  pages   cm
    ISBN 978-1-137-27969-9 (hardback)
    1. Education, Higher—Aims and objectives—United States. 2. Universities
and colleges—United States. 3. Higher education and state—United States.
4. Educational change—United States. I. Title.
LA227.4.C73   2015
378.001—dc23
                                                                2014029034

Design by Letra Libre, Inc.

First edition: March 2015

10 9 8 7 6 5 4 3 2

Printed in the United States of America.

CONTENTS

ACKNOWLEDGMENTS

WHILE MUCH OF THIS BOOK COMES OUT OF THE *University Ventures Letter,* a higher education biweekly publication that has circulated for the past three years, many ideas go back much further. Between sophomore and junior years at Yale in the summer of 1992 I was writing about the exorbitant growth in administrative spending at Yale ("The Bloating of the University") for my tabloid newspaper, *Rumpus,* with the assistance of several helpful librarians at Sterling Memorial Library. As a senior in the spring of 1994 I was lucky enough to work with Professor Joel Waldfogel on a paper that compared the Canadian and US university systems and ended up winning an Economics Department prize. Even then I had the strong sense that while college was supposedly equipping us with analytical skills and an inquisitive mindset, few were setting their sights on higher education itself.

I owe a great deal to media entrepreneur Peter Price for helping me see the business opportunities in higher education, particularly in online education. Peter's indefatigable enthusiasm for how technology will transform higher education for the good has stuck with me and is a core theme of this book. I'm also forever indebted to Ann Kirschner and Michael Crow (formerly at Columbia, now at CUNY and Arizona State, respectively) for trusting me with Columbia's good name and reputation as we tried to make our way through the fog of the early Internet. David Wolff accompanied me on that early journey, kept me sane and remains a good friend.

My experience as an investor in education is entirely due to the unwarranted confidence shown in me by Rod Moorhead and Steve Distler at Warburg Pincus. I learned so much from both of them. While at Warburg, I had the honor of working with Lance Odden, long-time head of the Taft School, and a giant in the field. As my focus shifted to higher education, I worked with a number of superb investment professionals at Warburg, led by Pat Hackett and including Greg Back, Mark Colodny, Justin Sadrian, Bob Pringle and Mimi Strouse. While at Warburg, I enjoyed many stimulating discussions about the future of higher education with Howard Newman and Bill Janeway. It was at Warburg that I first met Roger Novak, who remains a mentor and role model. Thanks as well to Elliot Sainer at Aspen Education Group for his partnership and friendship.

I learned a great deal from the founding and growth of Bridgepoint Education, much of which is incorporated here. Thanks to Andrew Clark for conveying his vision so convincingly, as well as for ignoring the elements of my vision that clearly weren't going to work. Thanks to Scott Turner, Wayne Clugston, and David VandePol for trusting us with Charter Learning. I'm deeply grateful to the founding Bridgepoint management team for their commitment and execution: Dan Devine, Chris Spohn, Rocky Sheng, Jane McAuliffe, Ross Woodard and Charlene Dackerman. It's been wonderful learning from Diane Thompson, Tom Ashbrook, Doug Abts and Raj Kaji over the past few years, as well as from board members Bob Hartman and Dale Crandall. Finally, through Bridgepoint, I have benefited a great deal from getting to know Adarsh Sarma and Ian Chiu, my more able successors at Warburg and investment professionals of the highest integrity and ability.

These experiences culminated in the establishment of University Ventures (UV). Daniel Pianko joined with me to establish what we dreamed would become the premier platform for innovation and capital in higher education. University Ventures aims to partner with traditional colleges and universities to help them navigate the disruption underway. Three years in, we are achieving what we set out to do: establishing a wide range of programs that improve return on investment for students. Daniel has been a constant source of ideas and support on this journey. Thanks as well to Tatiana Goldstein, Gregg Rosenthal, Aanand Radia, Ankit Dhir, Marissa Strong, our very able counsel, Larry Kane, at Orrick, Herrington & Sutcliffe. And special thanks to Dave Figuli for co-founding the firm with us. Dave remains an incredible source of ideas and inspiration.

UV wouldn't exist without the strong support of our limited partners (LPs). The global media and services company Bertelsmann was our first LP. This is as a result of the vision of Thomas Rabe whose partnership we hold dear. Chris and Shobna Mohn are also exceptional partners with a commitment to always taking the right path in higher education. Thanks as well to Bertelsmann executives involved with UV: Jörn Caumanns, Kay Krafft, Markus Dohle, Fernando Carro, Judith Hartman, Hays Steilberg, Chris Rosenbaum, Susanne Erdl, Bettina Wulf, Gail Rebuck, Thomas Mackenbrock, Pankaj Makkar, Michael Bouri, as well as Jörg Draeger at the foundation. Dalia Das has been of special assistance to UV, although—as I've tried to teach her and other native German speakers at Bertelsmann—not special as in "special education."

I want to thank Lindel Eakman and Lara Jeremko at UTIMCO for their commitment to higher education. Their level of engagement and effectiveness has been remarkable and they are two of my favorite people. I'm also very grateful to Jon Sackler, Brian Olson, Brian Piacentino and Donald Hawks III for their support and commitment to education reform.

Matt Greenfield and Stewart Greenfield were early supporters, and Matt remains a true comrade in arms. Further thanks are due to Trace Harris at Vivendi for sharing our vision, as well as to Jamie Merisotis, Dave Maas and Eileen Scott at Lumina Foundation, to Bill Hansen, Steve Ham, Mark Pelesh and Leonard Gurin at USA Funds, to William Louis Dreyfus, Jeffrey Gilman and Yoji Nimura, to Josh Susser at ECMC, and to Mac Narahara, Amit Avnet and Peter Waller at Mitsui.

Each *UV Letter* generates feedback that is always constructive and enjoyable and often provides ideas for the next missive. I deeply appreciate the contributions of everyone involved in this dialectic: Peter Enestrom, James Liu, Mac Hofeditz, Shannon Zoller, Marty Waters, Phil Obbard, Dvora Inwood, Jenna Talbot, Ben Wallerstein, Joe Rourke, Collin Gutman, and my three boys—Leo (8), Hal (5) and Zev (3), who inspire me to yell, laugh and write (typically in that order).

Many of the ideas in this book are derived from or inspired by work being pursued by our portfolio companies. I'm grateful for their leadership: Norm Allgood, Paul Gleason, Bob Haimes, Clay Gillespie, Scott Wenhold, John Donohue and Lowell VandeKamp at Synergis Education; Gene Wade, Kathleen Farley, Brian Newman, Eric Russell, Sal Monaco, Emily Chiu and Janet Holmgren at UniversityNow; Nicos Peristianis, Christos Vlachos, Nicos Nicolaou, Andreas Polemitis, Antonis Polemitis, Andreas Charalambous, Odysseas Christodoulou and George Soleas at EDEX; Dave Lenihan, Carlos Rojas and Ann Cass at Ponce School of Medicine; Jim Deters at Galvanize; Tony Digiovanni, Lizy Lamboy, Celina Ponce and Rebekah Lee at Ameritas; and Satish Menon, Joseph Deck, Tomi Blinnikka, Jayakumar Muthukumarasamy and Gina Dorst at TrueNrth who helped me to understand The Great Unbundling. Thanks are also due to Geoff Webster, Sharon MacDonald, Tom Bird, Linda de Lay, John Watson, Arlene Stewart, Michael Stewart and Fiona Crosbie at Metis.

ACKNOWLEDGMENTS

I'm very grateful to the many leaders in higher education who have spent time with me discussing the ideas in this book: Mike Crow, Phil Regier, Julia Rosen and the leadership at Arizona State; Jim Doti at Chapman and Gary Brahm at Brandman; Sebastian Thrun at Udacity; former Secretary of Education Margaret Spellings; Michael Horn at the Clayton Christensen Institute; former Undersecretary of Education Sara Martinez Tucker; Dan Greenstein, Josh Jarrett and Jason Palmer at the Gates Foundation; Gib Hentschke and Jon Barnett at USC; Sabrina Kay at Fremont College; Stephen Lassonde at Harvard; Joe May at the Dallas Community College System; Gerry Heeger, formerly of University of Maryland University College; Parminder Jassal at the ACT Foundation; Michael Brophy at California Marymount University; Louis Soares at ACE; Mitch Kapor at Kapor Capital; Ben Polak, Lucas Swineford and Diana Kleiner at Yale; Charles Bullock at Brandman; Paul LeBlanc at Southern New Hampshire; Wayne Smutz at UCLA Extension; Jamai Blivin and Merrilea Mayo at Innovate+Educate; Karan Khemka at Parthenon; Corey Greendale at First Analysis; Trace Urdan at Wells Fargo; Tony Miller and Phil Alphonse at Vistria; Teri Cannon; Bob Dickeson; and Michael Moe and Deborah Quazzo at GSV.

Thanks are also due to Carole Mann for so ably representing the book, and to Karen Wolny, Lauren Lo Pinto, Alan Bradshaw and Roberta Melville at Palgrave Macmillan for believing that what I had to say was of value and for not editing out all my crazy analogies and stories. I deeply appreciate all their work and support in guiding and forming this book.

On a personal note, I'm forever indebted to my grandparents who made it possible for me to attend Yale. Without the love and support of Lou and Estelle Craig, I would have gone down a completely different path. And it's worth noting that although my mother and father are extremely different people, they united for a bright, shining moment during the grooviest period in human history to make me and my brother. I can't speak for my brother (he never lets me), but as an investor in higher education, I'm clearly the product of my community college professor mother and my entrepreneur father.

Most of the stories in this book involve or are inspired by the antics of my wonderful brother Aaron (without whom life would be much less fun and interesting), my best friend Dave Friedman (in whose amazing brain the antics invariably originated), and my college roommates and *Rumpus* co-founders: Chris Douvos, Alex Sion and Chris Corrie. My friends, the summer is not yet over. I'm also indebted to the original members of Book-World: Jon Busky, Michael Saul, Tom Shakow, Josh Goren, Kevin Ryan, Rich Chin, Michael Lerner, Bill Baxter and Eric Siegel.

My sister, Laurel Waterman, served as my researcher, first reader, line editor and constant companion on this book in the midst of giving birth to her daughter, Althea. When she's not giving birth, she's a faculty member at University of Toronto. She's also one of the most brilliant and beautiful people I know. I was honored to partner with her on this book. I hope she's as proud of it as I am of her.

Finally, this book is dedicated to my wonderful, patient and loving wife, Yahlin Chang. I'm blessed to share my life with her. Although she never earned a graduate degree, according to a prize she received upon her graduation from Yale in 1994, she apparently made various and sundry "contributions to the intellectual life of Branford College." The framed award proudly hangs today over our kitchen garbage can.

Ryan Craig
January 2015

COLLEGE
DISRUPTED

ONE

BUNDLE OF JOY?

IT WASN'T UNTIL I WAS 14 THAT I GAVE A THOUGHT to US universities. Growing up in Toronto, Canada, in the 1980s, the practice at my high school was not to think about university until the final year—the amusingly named Grade 13—when you'd receive a one-page form with the names of all 15 universities in the Province of Ontario and were asked to rank your top three choices. No standardized tests, prep courses or college counselors. No campus visits or interviews required. You'd simply record your preferences and the schools would either accept or reject you on the basis of your transcript, appended to the form.

But then I heard about a nerd in Grade 13 who, without telling anyone, applied and was accepted at Princeton. Everyone was abuzz about this nerd. If we thought about university at all, it was about the relative merits of London, Ontario (Western University) versus Kingston, Ontario (Queen's University). There was no question about going to University of Toronto. That was for losers who wanted to live at home. Going to Princeton was like going to outer space.

Still, I remember thinking that if you were going to take the trouble to go to space (or "the States," as we called it), of course you'd only do it for an Ivy. What else was there in the States? And if there were other universities, surely they'd want to be like Princeton. Little did I know this notion was at war with what really makes American higher education great.

My first job made an even bigger impression. One Sunday morning that spring I awoke at a friend's apartment following a "sleepover" (a night of playing videogames, looking at *Penthouse* and drinking alcohol) feeling shiftless. I had spent the prior evening sober, helping less sober friends on and off subway cars without falling onto the tracks or attracting official notice.

That morning I completed job applications at two establishments: Baskin-Robbins and Oliver's Restaurant. B-R called me for an interview that afternoon. Later that week I started my first shift as a trainee. We were permitted to bring home a quart after every shift. Bringing home those quarts filled me with pride and my freezer with ice cream. My ice cream adventure lasted less than a month; Oliver's called, interviewed me and hired me as a busboy. No longer would I work for the minimum wage. Now I would earn minimum wage plus tips.

Busing tables at Oliver's was the formative experience of my adolescence. I learned two important things there. First, no matter what food got dumped into the large bins we called "bus pans," the "bus juice" at the bottom invariably had the same dark gray coloring and the same sickly sweet smell. Second, and derivative of the first, I needed to go to a good university.

Most waiters at Oliver's had attended Canadian universities. While we made work as fun as possible, it was a large and busy restaurant: 8-hour shifts could extend to 10 or 11 hours depending on the traffic. Twenty-five years later, I still have nightmares of an empty section being seated in unison: 15 tables clamoring for drinks, bread and rolls and wanting to order. After the shift, we'd pull tables together in an empty section and commiserate. The waiters and waitresses would smoke and down a few bottles of Labatt Blue beer and tell stories. Then they'd take off their filthy, food-coated black sneakers (black so they'd look like dress shoes), store them in their lockers and take the subway home.

Ambition has many mothers; mine was fear. I saw my future waiting tables. Though a great job during high school—providing ample pocket money so I could try to impress girls with elaborate presents (a mountain bike) and expensive dinners followed by tickets to *Les Misérables*—the idea of waiting tables without end in sight motivated me in a way I hadn't been motivated before. So I worked hard, did well in school and at the end of the decade, in the fall of 1989, my father drove me to the University of Toronto where I took the SATs—a prelude to a Christmas break in front of the typewriter working on applications—ultimately successful—to Brown and Yale.

Visiting Brown, somehow I ended up on the campus radio station. At Yale, it was pitchers of beer at Branford College's Naples Night, which galvanized me to lead other pre-frosh on a blind-leading-the-blind tour of Calhoun College's newly renovated basement. Brown was fantastic and the pizza was equally good. But at Yale, as they say, ELI: Everything Looked Impressive. I was hooked.

My first week at Yale that fall was the first time I heard a gunshot. It was 3 a.m. I was in bed (not my own). And I thought: Welcome to America. The danger of the place—my sophomore year, a student was shot and killed right in the middle of campus—caused students to turn inward, resulting in an unfathomable level of energy on campus. Fear of death begetting life, or at least a college version thereof. An unfortunate by-product of this fear was ignorance of other colleges and universities in town. Yalies might bump into students from Quinnipiac or Southern Connecticut State at Toad's Place, the campus concert venue. But we knew nothing about them or their institutions.

That all changed for me senior year with my economics senior essay. I realized my current set of job opportunities and relationship (girlfriend from New York who would become wife from New York) would likely keep me from returning home to Canada any time soon. I thought about killing two birds with one stone: complete the senior essay and eradicate any misgivings surrounding my decision to abandon the True North Strong and Free. And so with the support of my economics advisor, Professor Joel Waldfogel (then known nationally as the Grinch for his attempt to calculate the deadweight loss of Christmas), I set out to use econometric modeling to compare the Canadian and US higher education systems.

Assembling the Canadian data set was simple. There were 60 universities nationwide and data was available for all of them. Assembling the US data was much more time-consuming and eye-opening. I spent days in Sterling Memorial Library poring through university guides and *U.S. News* rankings. The scope and diversity of the system stunned me. I had no idea that the amount US colleges and universities spent annually per student varied by as much as $30,000 depending on the institution—over five times the level of variance in Canada. A world, once hidden, was now revealed. In conflating American higher education with the Ivy League, I was suffering from acute myopia.

MYOPIA CORRECTED

Twenty years on, I realize I was not the first or the last to be blinded by the Ivy League. America's colleges and universities are often referred to as "the wonder of the world" or a "crown jewel."[1] Such statements, typically made by wealthy and powerful people who attended schools like Yale and are quoted in places like the *New York Times*, are a product of the threshold challenge facing any serious discussion of the state and future of American higher education: myopia.

Here's a fun exercise. Try naming 50 colleges or universities that meet the following criteria:

- Their name doesn't include the name of a state
- They don't have Division I football or basketball teams

If you can't do this, you may have myopia. And welcome to the club. It often seems that the set of people most engaged in discussing the future of higher education and the set of people who attended top 50 schools are one and the same. Of course, the top 50 are no more representative of the whole than the top 1 percent of earners is of the American workforce.

A serious discussion of higher education requires a broader view and, accordingly, would benefit from broader participation. Let's start with the basics. The 6,000 Title IV–eligible colleges and universities in the United States employ over 3 million people and produce nearly $500 billion in revenue each year from over 20 million students, an increase of more than 30 percent from 15 years ago.[2] This enrollment growth is mainly the product of two things: the baby boom echo and the fact that the notion that college is the most direct path to a career and comfortable life is now as American as motherhood and apple pie. Which is why 70 percent of US high school graduates now partake in higher education—the highest level of matriculation in the world.

But taking a broader view also means looking beyond inputs to outcomes. The most obvious outcome is graduation rates. While graduation rates at the top 50 schools approach 90 percent, overall graduation rates hover around 55 percent for four-year institutions and 29 percent for two-year colleges. Some state universities graduate fewer than 25 percent of their students within six years of enrollment. According to the National Student Clearinghouse Research Center, more than 31 million students left higher education in the past 20 years without earning any credential. About one-third dropped out within the first term; 80 percent of the remainder dropped out within the first two years.[3] Higher education institutions blame the poor performance of our K-to-12 system which graduates students from high school who are not capable of college-level work. And 60 percent of entering community college students are relegated to remedial courses before being admitted to a degree program. But higher education is failing in its remediation efforts; over 70 percent of students in remedial math courses do not pass these courses. This means about 4 in 10 incoming community college students—almost 2 in 10 of all undergraduates and mostly minority students—never have a fair shot. Our system of higher education may have the highest level of matriculation, but it also has the lowest level of completion.

Other surprises for higher education myopics who try on a pair of corrective lenses for the first time: 70 percent of the 20 million students in the American higher education system are enrolled in public colleges or universities. The vast majority are enrolled at non-research-intensive state institutions—the beating heart of American higher education. Only 29 percent are what myopics picture when they think of college students (18-to-22-year-olds attending a four-year college or university on a full-time basis); 43 percent of students are over the age of 25.[4] Most of the rest are younger students who attend community colleges (45 percent of all undergraduates). So if *Animal House* is your paradigm for American higher education, the most typical student is John Belushi's Bluto: older, probably not attending full-time and not completing anytime soon.

Another surprise and an important contributor to low completion rates: one-third of students transfer at least once before graduating and 25 percent transfer more than once. So if you prefer to view the world through the lens of politics, give some thought to Sarah Palin, who attended five institutions before finally graduating, initially making an ill-informed decision to matriculate at University of Hawaii-Hilo because she wanted to enjoy the Hawaiian sunshine. (She had failed to do her due diligence: Hilo is on the rainy, volcanic side of the Big Island with fewer than 40 days of clear skies per year. She promptly transferred after her first semester.)

With this broader picture in mind, if America's colleges and universities truly are "the wonder of the world," it's not due to the achievements of the top 50 but rather a result of the system's diversity. It serves first generation immigrants with a GED, and—at the same time, typically but not necessarily at different institutions—it serves fifth-generation legacies (students whose parents or other family members attended the college). While higher education in almost every other country is public and fairly homogeneous across institutions, private institutions (from Harvard to St. Olaf College) play a major role in the US system, and public colleges and universities also embrace a high degree of heterogeneity. Clark Kerr's master plan for the University of California is the archetype for American public higher education, with the UC schools charged with enrolling the top eighth of high school graduates, the California State University system enrolling the remainder of the top third, and community colleges providing access to everyone else. As Arthur Levine remarked in his preface to *Higher Learning in America, 1980–2000*: "The importance of the California Master Plan was that it stopped the stampede toward a single, homogeneous model of higher education. Excellence, in many purposes was chosen over mediocrity . . ."[5]

American higher education is designed to produce excellence at top institutions while addressing accessibility at others. The result is the most diverse system of higher education in the world.

PERNICIOUS ISOMORPHISM

It would be nice if we could celebrate the diversity of higher education in America and call it a day. Through it, the system achieves both excellence and accessibility. But the myopia that obscures this diversity has also produced college rankings.

The *U.S. News* rankings and the other 14 rankings currently active in the United States are primarily derived from easy-to-measure inputs: student selectivity; faculty resources (class size, student to faculty ratio); spending per student; library holdings; and research productivity (an input into student learning). It may be tautologically risky to say it, but here goes: the top 50 do really well in these rankings. (So well, in fact, they tend to always finish in the top 50. And so consistently that *U.S. News* might as well rank colleges each year based on institutional age.) Why? Because the rankings are designed to measure what elite colleges do well: lavish money and resources on really bright, motivated students.

Trying to move up in the rankings is a Sisyphean task. A 2013 study published in the journal *Research in Higher Education* concluded that any sustained upward movement in rankings is nearly impossible. The paper, written by researchers from University of Rochester, asked what it would take for Rochester, a university consistently ranked in the mid-30s, to move into the top 20. The answer: Increase average faculty salary by $10,000 and spend $12,000 more per student. This would cost $112 million per year. And then Rochester would have to increase its graduation rate by 2 percent and improve in other metrics like alumni giving and acceptance rate.[6]

Nonetheless, driven by boards of elite trustees, university and college presidents navigate their institutions by the stars of these rankings. "No one in the United States tries to figure out what a great university is," says Andreas Schleicher, head of the education arm of the Organisation of Economic Co-operation and Development (OECD). "They just look at the Ivy League."[7]

To be fair, rankings are only one of the four Rs that now dominate the higher education landscape. The four Rs are:

- Rankings
- Research
- Real Estate
- Rah! (sports)

All are easy to measure and communicate to alumni and other development constituencies. And all have precious little to do with student outcomes. All also happen to be dominated by the top 50.

The result is isomorphism, the phenomenon by which American universities have acquired similar characteristics. R.R. Reno describes isomorphism in a piece he wrote for *First Things*:

> There aren't enough Nobel Prize winners to go around, so lesser universities chase the also-rans and young phenoms in the hope of gaining ground in the reputation race, offering them lighter teaching loads. To dampen the ill-will that arises when regular faculty began to envy the student-free lives of the academic heroes, the wealthier

universities have consistently moved toward across-the-board reductions in teaching loads, with not-so-wealthy schools imitating
this trend as best they can. This, of course, requires shifting still
more teaching to graduate students and other adjunct, non-tenured
faculty.[8]

The result is a uniform model of program delivery through which most
American colleges and universities aim to become "The Harvard of the
_____" (fill in the blank for the region). They attempt to offer the same
range of programs and provide the same services as an institution with an
endowment of nearly $30 billion. It's a recipe for the crises we'll explore in
the next few chapters.

Take a look at college catalogues from ten institutions chosen at random. What differences do you see? All claim to offer the same basic programs and experience with little differentiation other than an "international
focus," a "community service" experience, or a "values-based education."

A report released in the summer of 2014 by the New America Foundation made this point clearly. The purpose of the report was to criticize the
American Association of Universities (AAU), the premier association of
research universities. Written by policy director Kevin Carey, the report
correctly pointed out that the stature of AAU membership causes universities to fruitlessly waste time and money focusing on superficial measures of
research activity—none of which relate to return on investment for tuition-
paying students. Through the AAU, wrote Carey, a "tiny cabal of venerable
institutions has done more to shape and, increasingly, harm the cause of
higher learning in America than any other group one could name."[9]

Isomorphism in American higher education is so pernicious because
it's at war with the diversity that makes it wondrous: private and public;
traditional age and mature students; elite and open. Different institutions

do different things to benefit different types of students. The four Rs don't work so well for the other 5,950 colleges and universities. It's as though all retail stores have decided to stock goods that only the top 1 percent can afford to buy. Champagne and caviar for all!

THE (COSTLY) TRADITIONAL DEFENSE

We need to keep all this in mind in evaluating the need for higher education. First up: the traditional defense. College graduates can expect to make 85 percent more than high school graduates over a lifetime—depending on the study, up to $1 million more—and weathered the recession much better than high school grads.[10] The unemployment rate for college graduates? Only 4.5 percent.

Growth in demand for college graduates doesn't appear to be tapering. There will be 55 million job openings between now and 2020. According to experts, 35 percent will require at least a bachelor's degree and another 30 percent will require some college.[11] We're currently on track to fall short by at least 5 million educated workers. Moreover, there are already 4 million unfilled jobs in the United States. So it's hard to disagree with President Barack Obama when he says "every American will need to get more than a high school diploma."

Mapping GDP per capita vs. average educational attainment state-by-state shows an increasing correlation over time—to the point that it's now virtually a straight line from West Virginia to Connecticut. So it's not surprising when policy makers look for higher education to come to the rescue; "college completion = economic performance" has become a catechism in Washington, DC, and state capitals. The importance of higher education to America's future is now one of a handful of issues that Democrats and Republicans still agree on.

But we're falling behind other countries. While American adults were the best educated in the world in the 1970s, we're now number 16 in terms of degrees held by young adults (ages 25 to 34).[12] Moreover, we're standing still as the rest of the world passes us by. In every other developed country (except Germany and Israel) this generation is more educated than the last generation.[13]

This was the motivation behind President Obama's first higher education priority. At his first State of the Union, the president asserted that "by 2020, America will once again have the highest proportion of college graduates in the world."[14] This goal would require graduating 10 million more students by 2020, increasing the percentage of the adult population with degrees from 40 percent to around 55 percent.[15]

The cost of meeting this need: an extra $30 to $40 billion per year before accounting for tuition increases. That would be a 40 percent increase in state support for higher education—a level no state could afford, let alone all 50 states. This paradox—we must produce more college graduates but can't afford to—has resulted in college-educated thought leaders streaming out of ivory towers in search of change.

THE DYSTOPIAN COUNTERFACTUAL

This book is about the crises facing the world's greatest system of higher education. I'll start with the most fundamental—what I call the dystopian counterfactual.

What if 100 percent of the supposed benefits of higher education are a result of self-selection bias? What if the pool of individuals who earn college degrees would have demonstrated higher employment levels and incomes simply as a result of their initiative, talent and grit (without regard to whether they earned degrees)? If college graduates went back in time and did nothing of educational value and persevered at it for four years, would we still see the same economic outcome? What if colleges and universities are essentially a playpen for 18-to 22-year-olds; we put them in the care of patient college administrators until they become safe for the workforce?

To illustrate the thinking behind the dystopian counterfactual, let's look at a Gates Foundation–produced video that is a classic version of the gospel of higher education. And then we'll conjure up a dystopian version of the same video.

In 2009, the unemployment rate for high school dropouts was more than twice as high as it was for college graduates. But increasingly, even a high school education isn't enough. A student who earns a college degree or other credential beyond high school has a much better shot at a brighter future. The proof is in the numbers. The lifetime earning potential for a student with a bachelor's degree: $3.4 million. A high school degree: $1.8 million. A high school dropout: $1.2 million. In 1973, 28 percent of jobs required an education beyond high school. In 2007, 59 percent. By 2018, 63 percent of all American jobs will require some sort of education beyond high school. In real numbers that means American employers will need 22 million workers with postsecondary degrees. But research shows that if we don't do something about this problem, we'll fall short by 3 million graduates. The future of our young people and our country is at stake. We must educate our way to a better future.[16]

Now here's the dystopian version:

In 2009, the unemployment rate for high school dropouts was more than twice as high as it was for college graduates. But increasingly, even a high school education isn't enough. A student who earns a college degree or other credential beyond high school has a much better shot at a brighter future. This is because employers want to hire people who not only have the talent and grit to complete the multi-year project known as high school, but also have the initiative to apply to college, and the talent and grit to finish a second multi-year project. Although nothing they learn in high school or college is relevant to employers, and although resources deployed to higher education are mostly a deadweight loss to the economy (the exception being college sports, which are fun to watch), by 2018, 63 percent of American jobs are likely to be filled from this self-selected pool of college graduates—the economy's largest, most easily identifiable pool of prospective workers.

This type of thinking prompted PayPal co-founder and internet bon vivant Peter Thiel to label US higher education "a bubble in the classic sense" and earn a ton of free publicity (*60 Minutes,* a character on a hit HBO series) by creating Thiel Fellowships: $100,000 awards to 24 students with the best reasons for dropping out of college to pursue their entrepreneurial ideas.

Thiel and others argue that although every study of a college degree's value demonstrates a compelling lifetime return on investment, that correlation may not hold for certain groups (such as very high achievers) and may not continue to hold following the financial crisis—which seems to be the case as the data starts trickling in.

Thiel is not alone. Legions of naysayers, "end is nigh-ers," and entrepreneurs are targeting higher education as the next large industry to be disrupted. One thing is certain: While higher education hasn't faced tough questions in the past—like the most popular kid in class, he's always just smiled, thankful for the social promotion—we've entered a new era. If colleges and universities are to avoid being replaced by some creation of Silicon Valley, they're going to have to answer the question of what students are actually learning and demonstrate how their programs benefit students. In an era when more than one-third of college and university presidents say American higher education is heading in the wrong direction, and when 57 percent of Americans say higher education is not providing students with good value,[17] like Luke Skywalker in *The Empire Strikes Back,* American higher education will have to understand and come to terms with itself in order to counter the dystopian counterfactual.

This book is my attempt to shed a little light on this problem. I plan to use a few tales from my own college experience as points of reference. Sometimes I'll verge into popular culture for analogies. I hope you'll agree these stories are relevant, and if not, at least entertaining.

The next three chapters explore the three crises—(1) affordability; (2) governance; (3) data—that explain why our colleges and universities are currently a bundle of nerves more than a bundle of joy.

TWO

CRISIS OF AFFORDABILITY

THIS CHAPTER CALLS FOR THROWING OUT NUM-bers like Frisbees. Catch this one: In the fall of 2013, a survey of more than 400 small private and regional state institutions found that nearly half had fallen short of budget enrollment or net tuition revenue.[1] And this one: From 2010 through 2012, freshman enrollment at more than a quarter of US private four-year colleges declined 10 percent or more.[2] This one: A 2014 study from UCLA's Higher Education Research Institute revealed that the percentage of students attending their first choice institution had reached a 40-year low.[3] And finally this one: In October 2013, the percentage of 2013 high school graduates who enrolled in higher education was 65.9 percent—down from 70.1 percent only four years earlier.[4]

Why the budget shortfalls, declining enrollment, and lost dreams? The same wind propels each Frisbee: a Crisis of Affordability in American higher education. Current and recent students have amassed unprecedented debt loads. The average bachelor's degree recipient who has taken out student loans is carrying approximately $30,000 in debt,[5] and 26 million consumers have two or more open student loans on their credit report.[6] Since 1999 outstanding student loan debt has grown by 511 percent. It now exceeds $1 trillion—more than credit card debt.

President Barack Obama spent a surprising amount of time on the college affordability crisis in 2012 and 2013. Right before students headed back to campus in the fall of 2013, the president went on a college tour to focus attention on the issue. Speaking at the State University of New York at Buffalo in August 2013, President Obama said,

> At a time when a higher education has never been more important or more expensive, too many students are facing a choice that they should never have to make: Either they say no to college . . . or you do what it takes to go to college, but then you run the risk that you won't be able to pay it off because you've got so much debt. Now, that's a choice we shouldn't accept. And, by the way, that's a choice that previous generations didn't have to accept.

President Obama is absolutely right about this. While many baby boomers recall how they worked through college in order to cover tuition, this is no longer possible for the average student. Working at the minimum wage in the late 1970s, a typical student at a four-year college could pay her entire tuition by working 182 hours—a part-time summer job. In 2013, the same student at the same college at the present-day minimum wage would have to work over 991 hours (a full-time job for half the year) just to cover tuition while still finding additional resources to pay for living expenses (and finding the time to attend classes)![7] Even taking grants into account, average tuition is more than half the average pre-tax family income for low-income students.

Many Americans now say higher education fails to provide students with good value and 89 percent of US adults agree with the statement that "higher education is in crisis." Here are two comments from the heart of the Occupy Wall Street movement, which migrated onto college campuses as Occupy College. First, a student commenting on the "We Are the 99 Percent" blog:

> Today my sociology professor asked a class of 35–40 hard-working students at a respected public university how many of us expected to get a job after graduation . . . No one raised their hand. Then she asked how many of us had over $10,000 in student loans . . . Almost every hand in the classroom, including mine, shot up.

It's not just the paupers who are popping mad. *Fortune*'s Dan Primack asked these fundamental questions in a piece titled "The Next Occupation":

> Where is the university's responsibility to its customers? Hell, where is its responsibility to America? Isn't college designed to enhance a student's future well-being and, in turn, that of society at-large? How did it get corrupted to the point where higher education is the cause, rather than the solution, to so many of our collective ills?[8]

Primack's outrage is justified: More than other businesses, higher education institutions ought to have a higher level of responsibility to their customers. There is obviously a strong social purpose to education. But higher education is also a one-time purchase; there are few repeat customers. So it is more likely that the purchase decision is made in a context of asymmetric information: The institution knows or should know the fair value of the product, but the purchaser is fairly clueless.

THE PRICE IS NOT RIGHT

Higher education tuition has increased at double the rate of inflation for over 30 years. The overall price of higher education increased 600 percent between 1980 and 2010—more than any other major product or service. In the *Chronicle of Higher Education*'s database, more than half of all colleges and universities raised tuition in 2012–13 and 40 colleges raised tuition by 10 percent or more. To ascertain what's really happening, however, we need to segment institutions based on funding source.

First, let's look at the public colleges and universities that enroll 70 percent of students.

In 1975, the average state-supported institution could count on state funding for over 60 percent of its budget.[9] Since then, between 1980 and 2011, all states save Wyoming and North Dakota have slashed support for higher education by anywhere from 15 to 70 percent. Why? Because for most states it's the least bad choice.

Medicaid spending has gone from 10 to 24 percent of state budgets.[10] States had to either raise taxes or cut billions out of budgets. When taxes go up, that impacts 100 percent of the population. When K-to-12 funding is cut, that impacts a high percentage of the population. Relatively speaking, cutting higher education impacts a small segment of the population. As Richard Vedder, director of the Center for College Affordability and Productivity has noted: "Legislatures are starting to rethink higher ed. If they have a choice between funding for the elderly or subsidizing the upper-middle-class kid to go to college . . . subsidizing the middle-class kid to go to college is a lower priority."[11] A recent Gallup Poll reflects this view among the general population: While Americans say they value higher education, fewer than 40 percent think states should provide more support to colleges.

The clarity of the logic notwithstanding, the magnitude of cuts has been difficult to stomach. On a per-student basis, state funding of public colleges is at its lowest level since 1980. In almost half of the states, students now pay a larger share of the cost of a public education than the state does.[12] Continuing the trend lines, Colorado would cease any support for higher education by 2024, and 15 other states would reach this benchmark by 2050. American higher education has undergone a fundamental transformation from public good to private good.

The recession hit state institutions particularly hard. Currently, 31 states spend less in absolute terms on higher education than they did in 2009. Louisiana spent $1.7 billion in 2009, but only $1.1 billion in 2014. In Arizona, spending declined 24 percent. And even though 40 states increased funding in the 2014 budget year, it's not always as it seems. In Illinois, much of the increase went to pension funds, not to the classroom.[13]

Meanwhile, for reasons I explore in the next chapter, the cost of delivering higher education has increased dramatically—an increase paid for by higher tuition. Annual tuition increases at public institutions have been nearly triple the level of inflation over the past 20 years and during the recession many systems resorted to double-digit annual increases.[14] So the majority of the overall increase in America's tuition bill—and the $1 trillion in student debt—is directly attributable to states' defunding higher education.

Keep in mind that tuition increases are only one part of the affordability crisis. Many institutions are also raising fees outside the tuition bill. Indiana University-Bloomington introduced a $180 "temporary repair and maintenance fee" and then doubled it. At Southern Illinois University, freshmen were charged a one-time $150 "matriculation fee" for "orientation."[15] And Georgia's public universities introduced a "special institutional fee" of $1,088. At Georgia Tech for 2013–14, freshman fees totaled $2,392.[16]

In one respect, most state institutions should be commended, because when prices aren't raised, you get California during the Great Recession. In 2010, 137,000 California community college students were unable to get into a class they needed. A larger number were unable to apply for federal financial aid—not because Title IV funds ran dry, but because there weren't enough counselors to help students complete applications. A panel established by California community college chancellor Jack Scott recommended rationing courses based on a student's track record of remaining on a set programmatic pathway, rather than waltzing, wandering, stopping and starting.

Around the same time, one of California's most prominent community colleges—Santa Monica College, which eliminated more than 1,000 class sections between 2008 and 2011—announced it would establish a two-tier pricing structure. Their tuition was $46 per credit. They planned to set the new pricing tier at $180 per credit, which would come into play once budgeted sections were filled; those willing to pay the higher fees would be permitted to enroll, and the college would open up additional sections. The result: rallies, pepper spray, an emergency meeting of the school's board and a shelving of the controversial plan.[17] However, other California community colleges have since adopted similar two-tier pricing structures.

As higher education moves from a public good to a private good, there are two choices: increase prices and supply or ration limited (public-supported) supply. Rationing is a hard word, evoking "death panels" in health care, but it is hard to deny that rationing occurred in California during the recession. California's public colleges continued to maintain low price points when demand vastly exceeded supply. Interestingly, the University of California (UC) system has avoided the fate of California State University and California's community colleges because it has not bound itself to a single, low price point. By aggressively recruiting out-of-state students who pay market-level tuition, UC institutions have rationed the subsidy itself and increased capacity rather than rationing a limited number of classroom seats.

Of course, this option isn't available to institutions that can't attract out-of-state students. It also has some unintended consequences, like the fact that students at the University of Texas have been encouraged by the financial aid office to buy plots of land in West Texas in order to establish residency.

In Boulder, Colorado, two companies, Tuition Specialists and In-State Angels, marketed "relocation" services to Colorado University students, promising to do all the "heavy lifting" to help nonresidents switch to in-state status. In 2010, 1,389 out-of-state students filed petitions to be granted in-state status, and 90 percent were granted. The sharp decline of nonresident undergraduates prompted the university to change tuition policy, requesting more information, such as bank statements and tax returns, to prove financial independence from their parents and in-state status. Now, Tuition Specialists is no longer in business, and In-State Angels is changing direction.[18]

Of course, a better option than rationing the state subsidy or raising tuition is reducing spending. This is a fundamental aspect of the Crisis of Governance I discuss in the next chapter.

PRICE DISCRIMINATION

Colleges are a bit like funeral homes.
Talking about getting your money's worth strikes some as a little crass.
—Rick Wartzman, writing on The Drucker Exchange

As for the private, not-for-profit colleges and universities that enroll 20 percent of students, they haven't increased tuition as quickly as public and for-profit schools, but they are only bested by airlines in terms of price discrimination.

Price discrimination means setting the sticker price as high as possible and then discounting as required on a student-by-student basis, to drain every last dollar from students.

In 2011–12, 123 private schools listed annual tuition, fees, room and board totaling more than $50,000. In 2012–13, 151 did, and Sarah Lawrence College was the first to break the $60,000 level. For the 2014–15 academic year, Sarah Lawrence is at $64,380. Tuition hikes also continued at more affordable institutions.

But, as the *Chronicle of Higher Education* asks, "affordability goes beyond sticker price, which most students don't actually pay. How should families think about college affordability? . . . At many colleges, almost no one pays the sticker price."[19] Or as Peter Sacks, author of *Generation X Goes to College,* states: "The published prices of higher education are virtually meaningless. The far more important number is net price, which is the cost of attendance (tuition sticker price plus expenses) less federal, state and, especially, institutional grants." Indeed, the average discount for freshmen at private colleges is now 42 percent.[20] And while the numbers are murky, there are indications that net prices at private institutions haven't risen nearly as quickly as sticker prices.

The good thing about price discrimination for colleges and universities is that those few who can afford to pay $50,000 or $60,000 per year may be asked to do so. Still, two very negative results of price discrimination give reason to stop and question this core tenet of private college pricing.

First, price discrimination is not fair. Over the last decade, merit-based aid increased more than need-based aid as colleges tried to attract more capable students. By 2008, a larger portion of students were receiving merit aid than need-based grants.[21] This trend has been tempered somewhat by the recession, with need-based aid overtaking merit aid. But there is still a shortage of need-based aid.[22] In addition, colleges use different formulas to award need-based grants. Some colleges consider home equity; others do not. Some students consider the assets of both divorced parents; others do not. All colleges award grants based on the family's finances from the previous year—also not always representative of a family's true financial situation. Finally, as the *Chronicle* has noted, "families can spend four years preparing and have four weeks to decide with all the information" once colleges respond with grant awards.

Second, ridiculous private college sticker prices sustained by price discrimination reduce college accessibility for lower income and minority groups regardless of what grants or discounts might be available. In the 2004 study, "Cost, Quality and Enrollment Demand at Liberal Arts Colleges" in the *Economics of Education Review,* economists at Berkeley and Reed demonstrated that price discrimination in higher education reduces quantity demanded: "Increasing both tuition and average grant levels by one dollar leads to a reduction in enrollment yield. Students appear to look beyond a 'net cost' number and consider tuition and aid separately. Perhaps this reflects uncertainty about continuation of aid in future years, whereas '[high] tuition is forever.'"[23]

Other economists have linked high sticker prices and price discrimination in higher education to confusion among low-income, non-English-speaking and first-generation students—confusion that discourages students from even applying to college. In a 2005 report by the Lumina Foundation, Jerry Sheehan Davis concluded: "One of the unintended consequences of tuition discounting is that financial access to four-year colleges for lower income, financially needy students may generally be diminished . . . Tuition discounting works for some colleges . . . but the actions by large numbers of individual colleges, when combined across all institutions, have produced some worrisome outcomes for students and for colleges in general."[24]

The unfairness and inaccessibility become apparent in thinking about how airlines would act if they price discriminated in the same way as private colleges and universities. A typical travel experience would go something like this: You are planning a trip; you send ticket requests to several different airlines that all charge a fee you know you would never pay; then a short period of time before you need to travel, the airlines respond with the discounts they're willing to give you, all based on different factors; you decide if you're going to fly, and if so, on which carrier. Such a model would ground American air travel and is at risk of grounding non-elite private colleges with sky-high sticker prices.

Finally, at the private sector or for-profit institutions that enroll approximately 10 percent of students, one key driver of tuition increases has been the increasing cost of acquiring students, particularly in online programs. This is a result of increased competition for key search terms. In essence, tuition increases at these institutions are funding Google profits. For the typical private sector online program, enrolling a new online student now requires spending $2,000 to $3,000 in advertising. As 50 percent of online students typically drop out within the first six months, that's $4,000 to $6,000 to acquire one "revenue-generating" student. So, few for-profit institutions can afford to limit tuition increases. In the past several years, most have resorted to the price discrimination practice mastered by their traditional brethren—keeping list prices high and then discounting on a student-by-student basis.

Overall, tuition increases have been to America's colleges and universities as oil and gas resources are to countries like Nigeria, Venezuela and Russia. The so-called natural resources curse states that countries with easy access to natural resources don't develop the requisite governance, institutions or competitiveness in other economic sectors. In higher education, at least up until 2009, the "plenty" was the seeming willingness of students to pay more for degrees. The "curse" is thousands of noncompetitive institutions.

Only a handful of institutions have been brave enough to counter the trend. Belmont Abbey, a Catholic college located on the outskirts of Charlotte, is one of six colleges to have announced a reduction in sticker price over the past few years. William Thierfelder, president of Belmont Abbey, which cut tuition by 33 percent, told CNN "it seemed a little bit like madness . . . We were raising tuition each year, only to give it back on the financial aid side to help students be able to afford it." He went on to add that most students are so discouraged by the sticker price that they don't even consider applying to a school they think is beyond their family's means.[25] Another one of the six is University of Charleston, which reduced tuition by 22 percent. Edwin Welch, Charleston's president, said he "realized parents and families were now considering the overall price, not just the discount . . . Advertised price is driving middle-class students away." Welch pointed to the example of Sewanee, University of the South, which announced a reduction in sticker price the prior year and saw an increase in enrollment.[26]

Two other factors magnify the college affordability crisis.

Across colleges and universities of all flavors, credit transferability makes the affordability problem worse. Here's a Frisbee that should shock you: Students who earn an associate's degree actually graduate with 79 credits vs. the 60 they need. Students who earn a bachelor's degree end up with 136 credits vs. the 120 that they need.[27] A recent study by the National Center for Education Statistics revealed that students who transferred from a regionally accredited institution lost an average of 12 credits, while students who transferred from a nationally accredited school lost 16 credits.[28]

Why is this? Because when a student transfers to a new college, the new college reviews every credit on the student's transcript, looks at the

Economics 110 course the student took and asks this question: Is this really equivalent to the Economics 110 course we offer at our institution? It doesn't help the student's cause that the ultimate decision maker at the new college is a faculty member—sometimes the very faculty member teaching Economics 110! The extra, mostly redundant credits mean more cost and time. That's more time for life to get in the way, meaning lower likelihood of completion and more debt.

And here's a second factor that's often overlooked: Tuition represents only half the cost of earning a bachelor's degree. According to a recent study by the Brookings Institution, the average US student spends $48,000 on tuition, but incurs an opportunity cost of $54,000 by going to school and not working full-time.[29]

THE COLLEGE PAYOFF

Q: How do you get an English major off your porch?
A: Pay him for the pizza

This is a joke I'm hearing more frequently these days. But the recession did a number on all majors, not only English majors. In 2011, 50 percent of college graduates under the age of 25 were jobless or underemployed. The median starting salary of graduates in 2009 and 2010 was down 10 percent from those who graduated before the recession.

Nearly 7 million young adults are neither in school nor working. Those who are working are more likely to be waiters, waitresses or bartenders than engineers, physicists, chemists and mathematicians (100,000 versus 90,000). According to *USA Today*, there were more college graduates working in clerical jobs, such as receptionist or payroll clerk, than in all computer professional jobs (163,000 versus 100,000).

More also were employed as cashiers, retail clerks and customer representatives than engineers (125,000 versus 80,000).[30] New studies showing that 15 percent of taxi drivers, 17 percent of bellhops and 5 percent of janitors have college degrees (up from 1 percent in 1970) do not inspire confidence in prospective students that an investment in college will pay off.[31]

The wealth gap between young and old is now wider than ever. The typical US household headed by a person age 65 or older has a net worth 47 times greater than a household headed by someone under 35.[32] This wealth gap is now more than double what it was in 2005. In all, 37 percent of young households have a net worth of zero or less—twice what it was 25 years ago.[33]

At the same time, published research continues to support the return on investment from a traditional college education, even for recent graduates. A recent Pew study reports the bachelor's degree vs. high-school-only annual income differential for millennials ages 25 to 32 to be $17,500.[34] Over a lifetime, that's close to $800,000. Still, there are increasing reasons to question this number and the idea of investing in just any bachelor's degree.

1) Dystopian Counterfactual Revisited

Millennials who have earned a college degree are more likely to be from supportive, wealthy, well-connected families. They're also more likely to be resourceful and have the stick-to-it-iveness that yields more remunerative employment. The typical result is they're no longer working at Starbucks by the time they turn 25—regardless of whether they have a college degree or not. While studies on twins with identical DNA and similar upbringing have shown that more education is correlated to higher income, they do not demonstrate that the more able twin wouldn't have made more money anyway.[35] No study has quantified the self-selection problem as a contributor to the income gap. But it is undoubtedly a major factor.

2) Dropouts Doing Worse

A recent study titled "The Economics of B.A. Ambivalence: The Case of California Higher Education" out of MIT and University of Minnesota–Twin Cities makes a convincing argument that any increase in the college–high school income gap since 1960 is a result of declining high school real income as opposed to increasing college income.[36]

3) Playing Russian Roulette

The same study demonstrates that enrolling in a bachelor's degree program is a risky decision—much riskier than a generation ago—as a result of skyrocketing tuition and student debt. In 1990, students graduating from California public colleges had virtually no chance of what the authors call "financial distress" (i.e., loan repayments larger than 15 percent of their income). Today, men graduating from California public institutions have a 38 percent chance of financial distress and women have a 55 percent chance.

Keep in mind that the Pew study calculating millennials' annual and lifetime income differential of college graduates does not account for student debt, income taxes or breaks in employment. Adding these to the equation, the average income gap may be as much as 65 percent lower (which would reduce the annual income gap to $6,000 and the lifetime gap to $275,000). It may be that college degrees are an overly expensive and an inefficient signal to employers.

In addition, as Lauren Asher, president of the Institute for College Access and Success, says, "averages don't tell the whole story." With all of the above factors, we have entered a new era of unprecedented variance in returns on bachelor's degrees. While degrees from elite institutions continue to generate high incomes and strong returns on investment and engineering graduates continue to do well—engineering majors are 12 of the top 15 degree programs in terms of starting salary—other degrees from lower-tier institutions are producing net negative returns for students. Almost half of all college graduates have a job that doesn't require a bachelor's degree.[37]

The fundamental problem is that while only a minority of students enrolled in higher education are 18-to-22-year-olds who are full-time students at four-year institutions, the pricing of such programs has set something of a floor for the industry. But unless you're attending an elite university, the goal should be to avoid paying more for a non-STEM bachelor's degree than you absolutely need to. Otherwise you're the sucker paying double or triple the cover charge to get into the cool club and then not having any money left for drinks.

All of the above is exacerbated for the nearly half of American students who matriculate at our colleges and universities but don't complete. At some community colleges, graduation rates are below 10 percent. What this means is that students are incurring debt and, while they may be building skills through their coursework, it's unlikely they'll see any material return from their investment in higher education.

So it shouldn't be surprising that willingness to take on debt is at an historic low, and that students are starting to turn away from our colleges and universities. For many students, fear of debt now exceeds the fear of not having a degree.

THE CANARY IN THE HIGHER ED COAL MINE

To get a sense of what the future might look like for American higher education, take a look at law schools.

When I attended law school in the late 1990s, it already seemed expensive for the value being provided. I remember doing the math at the time. Students took four classes each semester and paid nearly $20,000 in annual tuition. The average class had about 50 students. So that's $125,000 tuition revenue per class. The average faculty member—not heavily burdened—would teach 1.5 classes each semester. So that's $375,000 in annual revenue per average faculty member, who (then) was probably being paid $125,000. The surplus went to administration, admissions, a costly renovation that disrupted students' lives and resulted in removal of the library from New Haven to Bridgeport, and—to try to make it up to us—a weekly Friday cocktail party in the dining hall with a keg of beer and greasy hors d'oeuvres. It also went to the university. Every university views its law school as a profit center contributing a significant portion of surplus back to the university's general budget.

I'm still not sure whether I've gotten any return on my law school investment. It's true that my sense of value may not only have been influenced by the horrific renovation, but also by my decision to concentrate in courses titled "_____ and the law," where the blank was something like "music," "sports," "television," "cyberspace" (and—most useful—"education") as well as my prior decision to avoid the practice of law at all costs.

I also constantly tested the limits of "value." I learned that the law school would pay the same salary to students who pursued public interest legal work over the summer as firms pay to summer associates. The work could be anywhere in the United States, so I took the law school's money and spent the summer working for the Legal Aid Society of Hawaii. I learned a lot that summer, but not so much about law.

And when it became known that the law school would gladly fund and host just about any student-initiated conference on a legal topic, my roommate Dave and I decided we would create the first-ever conference on Maple Syrup and the Law, exploring the array of complex legal issues facing the maple syrup industry. We withdrew our proposal when it became clear we were being taken seriously and would be burdened hosting a group of Vermont and Quebecois law faculty and students, all hopped up on maple syrup.

Finally, as a salute to Yale Law School, on every tuition check I noted in the memo section that the payment was one payment in a "series of bribes for JD degree."

I had no doubt that each check would be cashed. And it was, without incident.

Today, law schools are the canaries in the higher education coal mine. While average tuition at private law schools doubled in the past 15 years and nearly tripled at public schools, following the recession and massive cutbacks at law firms, law became the first large programmatic area in which the majority of graduates were clearly unable to achieve an adequate return on their tuition investment. Add to the recession other changes in the legal profession (i.e., the rise of offshoring and online self-help legal services) and the results are predictable: 45 percent of law school graduates unable to find a job that actually requires a JD degree; private law school graduates with an average debt of $125,000; unemployed graduates suing their schools over misleading placement data; two successive years of 20 percent declines in applications. In 2004, 100,000 students applied to law school. In 2013, only 59,400 did, the lowest number since 1977 and a 33 percent drop from 2010. First-year enrollment at law schools is down 25 percent from 2010 to 2013; 51 percent of law schools have cut the size of their entering classes.[38] Meanwhile, there were more than twice as many law graduates (46,565) as estimated job openings (21,640).[39]

Expect to see dozens of law schools close in the next decade. Hundreds of colleges and universities won't be far behind. A key hallmark of survivors (among non-elite institutions) is that they won't mind being a little crass in talking about how students are getting their money's worth. That means talking about the entire cost: tuition, fees, extra credits, opportunity cost, and the risk of dropping out and not receiving anything of value. It also means organizing the institution in a way that promotes delivery of high-return programs.

And so higher education governance comes to the fore.

THREE

CRISIS OF GOVERNANCE

THERE WAS A POPULAR SAYING AT ONE OF MY prior companies. Whenever someone came up with an idea that was less than grand, we'd say that person was a candidate to appear on the cover of *Bad Judgment Magazine*.

The company, Wellspring, was the leading organization of summer camps and boarding schools for treating childhood obesity. At one all-girls camp in upstate New York, the executive director and her senior team were feeling creative and made several faux *Bad Judgment Magazine* covers for staff training as vivid illustrations of what NOT to do at camp. The covers featured images of counselors at the supermarket loading up on junk food, sleeping together and drinking beer, along with "Survivor Story: I intentionally flipped my canoe!" and "The Dark Side of Arts and Crafts."

If I ever have the resources to launch this vanity publication, the cover of vol. 1, no.1 will have a photograph of a university board of trustees meeting. A 2011 Public Agenda survey of college and university trustees revealed that only a small minority of trustees took positions that were critical of administrators, and a majority of trustees said their primary source of information was the president. One trustee said: "It's an honor to be on the public board, but it's an honor that tends to accrue to people in the later stages of life, after they've already achieved some kind of prominence at some usually unrelated discipline . . . Trustees don't really want to spend the substantial time it takes to get up to speed on issues to the point where they can actually debate with an officer at the college." Another: "University trusteeships are sought-after positions because there are benefits that go along with it, and you've got people there for all the wrong reasons . . . You don't have people sitting on these boards who are really interested and engaged in making change."[1]

In short, trustees aren't asking the fundamental questions fiduciaries should ask. And it's not their fault. College and university boards are not built to question the assumptions that inform the proposals they approve.

TWO POINTS OF FAILURE

Higher education governance is failing for two reasons: unclear objectives and the shared governance model.

The first failure, unclear objectives, is a flaw common to all not-for-profit organizations (ironic, given the amount of attention paid in recent years to governance failures in for-profit higher education).

Americans rely on for-profit companies to provide most of our goods and services. We don't often question that wisdom. For-profit companies have a clear objective, a single bottom line. And the potential for abuse is obvious: scrimp on quality and increase profits. But maximizing profits today may mean no profits tomorrow. In striking this balance, directors of for-profit companies are crystal clear on what they're optimizing. This is the ultimate governor of profit maximization.

Consider addled Mrs. Lovett from the Stephen Sondheim musical *Sweeney Todd*. Mrs. Lovett's meat pie shop is a textbook example of poor corporate governance. To maximize her profits, Mrs. Lovett grinds all available proteins—cats, rats, roaches, and then Sweeney Todd's victims—and mixes them into her meat pies. But the bottom line, for-profit objective is not solely to maximize current profits, but rather to maximize the present value of the stream of profits into the future. Mrs. Lovett's "popping pussies into pies" may be good for her business today, but it does not make for a happy ending (for her customers, her business, or Mrs. Lovett herself).

Like all directors of not-for-profit organizations, university trustees are in a different boat. There is no single indicator or variable they are clearly maximizing or optimizing. That's because there is no single objective for the organization. Missions tend to be multifaceted, complex, and likely vague. Sometimes there's a double-bottom line. Often, there are so many bottom lines, there's really no bottom line at all. This makes it difficult for not-for-profit directors to ascertain whether management is doing a good job and to exercise appropriate governance. And it makes it easier for management to run the show and treat the board as its plaything. Which means the board isn't accountable to anything or anyone. Which leads to the cover of *Bad Judgment Magazine*.

The tragedy at Penn State is a good example. The failure of successive layers of university officials to report an assistant football coach who had been witnessed sexually abusing young boys is unfathomable for an institution whose mission is to develop young people. And yet, public and not-for-profit institutions do not have a single bottom line. So using very twisted logic, the Penn State officials who failed to take action against a known predator might have told themselves that they were protecting the football program, and that as the football program's health was integral to the institution due to the national attention, prestige and alumni support it attracts, protecting the assistant coach would serve Penn State's mission better than reporting him.

While this thinking is beyond the pale, what about a public or not-for-profit institution that admits and graduates underqualified student athletes? Or universities that commit to spend half a million dollars of general funds on tickets to a bowl game?

Second, the shared governance model, with multiple stakeholders and competing values, makes governance in higher education slower and more complex. Although faculty members have the privilege of sharing in governance, as Ann Kirschner, university dean of Macaulay Honors College of City University of New York (CUNY) says, "How many faculty even know the graduation rate of their students, or consider it their problem? . . . Faculty are rewarded as individual performers for their research and their contribution to the field, but have no incentive to reward institutional loyalty or accountability for student success."[2]

Most faculty members acknowledge shared governance is more of a brake on decision making, gumming up the works. Rarely do committees recommend anything contrary to administrators' priorities. But they always need to be consulted. In a *Chronicle of Higher Education* article, "Shared Governance Is a Myth," John Lachs writes about his experiences as chair of the Vanderbilt University Faculty Senate:

The chancellor met once a month with the senate's executive committee. The meetings were cordial, but it was clear that the chancellor used them to inform the senate of what he wanted. When the committee challenged some of his ideas, he summarily terminated the meetings, sending his provost to tell us each month what the chancellor had done.

On another occasion, I was asked to chair a committee assigned to develop a student bill of rights. The committee worked hard and came up with what seemed to many faculty members a balanced and sensible list of student rights and responsibilities. We were thanked for our labors—and then the document disappeared down a rabbit hole. No action has ever been taken pursuant to its terms, freshmen are not informed of its existence, and a search of Vanderbilt's publications turns up no reference to it.[3]

DEANLETS

Arguably the Crisis of Affordability is a consequence of the Crisis of Governance. But it's a somewhat distant relation. To better connect the dots, let's look at a trend for which the Crisis of Governance is a more proximate cause: the inexorable rise in spending on administration and noninstructional staff.

Between 1975 and 2005, colleges and universities increased the number of administrators by 85 percent, and the number of noninstructional staff by 240 percent.[4] From 2000 to 2012, the ratio of instructional to noninstructional staff declined an additional 40 percent.[5] At the University of Michigan, for example, there are 53 percent more administrators than faculty.[6]

Johns Hopkins professor Benjamin Ginsberg's 2011 book titled *The Fall of the Faculty: The Rise of the All-Administrative University and Why It Matters* coined the word "deanlet" to signify advanced degree holders who don't progress into academic positions, but begin working at universities as unnecessary staff and progress upward through the organization to become more highly paid unnecessary staff.[7] University board members defend the growth in noninstructional staff as due to increasing demand for technology and increasing regulatory compliance requirements. But the real reason, says Ginsberg—not entirely facetiously—is that bureaucrats naturally wish to expand themselves and so invent new work.

Many studies conclude that administrative bloat is a major cause of higher education's growing expense base.[8] A new study by the Institute for Policy Studies shows that at the universities with the highest paid presidents and chancellors, administrative costs grew twice as fast as scholarship spending.[9] Contrary to Ginsberg's conspiracy theory, presidents and trustees across the higher education landscape weren't sanctioning bloat for bloat's sake. Instead, each decision was ostensibly a rational response to perceived student and parent demands. As Patricia Leonard, vice chancellor for student affairs at University of North Carolina-Wilmington noted, faculty members don't deal with mental health, sexual assault or disabilities issues.[10]

FOUR Rs REVISITED

Rankings

Rather than being penalized for such spending, colleges and universities have been rewarded. *U.S. News* and other rankings evaluate colleges based on how much they spend per student. So it has seemed sensible to build up the administrative infrastructure, particularly if the deanlets could positively impact other rankings metrics: isomorphism in action. This has kept virtually every college and university from stepping back, looking at the big picture, and taking action to stem and reverse the growth in their cost base in order to address affordability.

Howard Bunsis, a professor at Eastern Michigan and chair of the American Association of University Professors' Collective Bargaining Congress, sees the increase in administration on every campus. "It's not what it should be," he says. "What's broken in higher ed is the priorities, and it's been broken for a long time."[11]

Real Estate

In the first issue of *Bad Judgment Magazine,* I envision an award-winning piece of photo-journalism featuring absurdly expensive college buildings. Many campuses today look like Disneyland. Suites are airy and well lit. Every room has broadband. Colleges are fully decked out with fitness centers, dance studios, and amenities more suited to cruise ships than universities. Students eat in dining halls serving all local, seasonal and sustainable food and employing menus designed by Alice Waters of Chez Panisse.

When I was at Yale, someone at some point had spent a lot of money on the place, but clearly not in the last 30 years. The buildings—onto which the architects had originally poured sulfuric acid to make them resemble, as one contemporary critic noted, "a stage-set for a musical about Oxford and Cambridge"—looked as though they couldn't bear another drop. Rooms were cramped, stuffy and overheated. As a rule, doors were unlocked or easily circumvented. So in a weird way, I feel sorry for students today. Because they have cable in their bedrooms, they'll never learn how to install a VHF antenna on the roof without setting off a fire alarm. That's a lesson my roommate Chris learned through trial and error (the error causing an evacuation of Vanderbilt Hall). They'll never run rampant up gothic towers and down steam tunnels, into the libraries and dining halls at night, and to cupolas to conduct science experiments involving cartons of iced tea and gravity. And because students now nibble on grass-fed beef burgers, they're missing out on the fried cheese that was the gastronomic highlight of our week.

My alma mater is not alone in this shift. The same forces that led to deanlets have created an arms race in facilities. In fall 2010, University of

Michigan opened the $175 million North Quad dorm that features a television production studio and two coffee shops. Down in Charlottesville, at another public flagship, University of Virginia spent $220 million on construction in 2011, including four new dorms.

The *New York Times* recently reported on the aquatic features built by universities. Texas Tech spent $8.4 million on a waterpark with a lazy river and waterslide. Auburn has developed a $52 million waterpark, including a 45-student paw-print-shaped hot tub and a 20-foot wet climbing wall. Pensacola Christian has put in a $1 million wave rider. North Dakota State is building a waterpark with a 36-foot vortex of swirling water, a fireplace on an island in the middle of a pool, a rain garden to mist lounging students, and a zip line atop it all. Clemson is developing a 38-acre lakefront property to include "blobs"—floating mattresses placed so students can jump on board "like [on] American Ninja," says the university's director of recreation. Louisiana State is building a lazy river that will spell out the letters LSU in the school's signature Geaux font. Missouri has a lazy river, waterfall, indoor beach club, and a grotto modeled after the one at the Playboy Mansion. Not to be outdone, Missouri State has put in a waterpark complete with zip line and lazy river, but insists on calling the lazy river a "current river" because Missouri State students are "not lazy." According to the *Times,* 92 universities are reporting over $1.7 billion in recreation center projects. Texas Tech paid for its waterpark with an increase in student fees. Auburn raised its student activity fee from $7.50 to $200 to fund its waterpark.[12]

Out in California, University of California-Los Angeles spent $5.1 million to open a dining hall that offers exclusively Asian food from China, Japan, Thailand, Vietnam, Korea, India and Hawaii, pairing two cuisines at each meal. UCLA chefs designed the menu after visiting leading ethnic restaurants across Southern California. They now serve up dishes like spinach and seaweed rolls, Indian potato croquettes, Buddha's delight, and Japanese soba noodles with asparagus; students can wash these dishes down with Korean ginger and rice punch. In case students don't realize this isn't typical cafeteria fare, they are welcomed by hosts in several Asian languages and video screens broadcast cable news shows from Japan, South Korea and India. The renovation allowed UCLA to install a stone oven for flatbreads. To ensure students in the heartland don't miss out, the University of Missouri launched a dining hall where chefs prepare each student's order individually. Back at Michigan, the new North Quad has been awarded gold status by the National Association of College and University Food Services for its salmon filet, tortellini with walnut pesto sauce, lamb and even shark (one hopes, not from Lake Michigan).

It's not difficult to find apologists for such extravagance. UCLA's residential food and beverage director calls today's college students "much more food savvy. They are used to going out to eat and more used to restaurant environments and restaurant quality of food." The dining services director at University of Kansas says "experiencing good food in a nice setting can influence a student's choice of a college and continuing relationship with it." And at UVA, the director of facilities ponders "the big question of how is it that students learn? Is it just the classroom, or is it in the halls between classes? Or is the environment part of the teaching tool? I would say the environment is part of the teaching tool, and Mr. Jefferson felt that very strongly."[13]

How does a lazy river advance learning outcomes, even for oceanography majors? It's easier for students, their parents, alumni and trustees to compare shower fixtures or dining hall menus than organic chemistry curricula (let alone learning outcomes themselves). Even community colleges, which aren't known for their facilities, aren't immune. In a recent article in the *Chronicle of Higher Education*, Kim Linduska, executive vice president at Des Moines Area Community College, defended her institution's effort to build housing: "As community colleges have grown and matured, many more of them have worked harder to attract students." In Indiana, Ivy Tech Community College in South Bend recently completed a $4.5 million dining hall and student center, and the campus in Gary is developing a $17 million fitness and wellness center. A performing arts center is also being contemplated. Meanwhile, Los Angeles Community College District is spending over $25 million building fitness centers, gyms, tracks and tennis courts.

With the Crisis of Affordability, dissenting voices are being heard. But these voices are more likely to be students than the trustees who marvel at their institutions' facilities and food. According to one UVA student quoted in the *Cavalier Daily,* "It's a misappropriation of funds. They're cutting classes, departments aren't funded well enough; they are sacrificing our education for the sake of getting more money from alumni." Whether or not they're sacrificing education, it sure increases the cost of education.

One of the few costs that have risen faster than tuition are other fees such as room and board. Richard Vedder, director of the Center for College Affordability and Productivity, has noted, "Universities are in the business of feeding, lodging, entertaining, and providing health care, and sometimes these activities absorb as many, or more resources as funds spent on teaching and research."[14] Clearly, as the report concludes, "more attention needs to be paid to cost control for these other expenses."

I was a beneficiary of great (albeit decaying) architecture and am not opposed to such when it doesn't increase costs. Great architecture can spark great ideas. Great meals can be the context for life-changing conversations. But nothing in higher education inspires more than actual learning.

Rah

Unfortunately, nothing in higher education inspires the general public (and especially alumni) more than Division I football and basketball. My experience in intercollegiate athletics was pretty much as far from Division I as you can get. I served as catcher of the Yale Law School softball team. We'd compete in the University of Virginia Law School softball tournament—the World Series of law school softball. Each participant received a package with welcome statements from the vice president, the governor, senators and congressmen. It was a convivial affair, at least until we had to play the team from University of Miami Law School. Those guys were built like Jose Canseco.

I now live in Los Angeles where, contrary to popular belief, there is a professional football team: the University of Southern California's Trojans. Attending a USC game recently was something of a fish-out-of-water, nun-in-a-brothel moment for me.

The numbers surrounding college athletics are as shocking as the scandals erupting weekly from big-time college sports. Division I schools with football spend over $90,000 per athlete on sports—seven times the average spending per student. Universities claim much of this spending is for additional student aid, but the data show only 16 percent goes to student aid, and 84 percent goes to athletic staff salaries, game expenses and—increasingly—pro-level facilities to attract top recruits. Total Division I sports revenue is $12 billion. The crazy thing is that universities lose money on sports and subsidize the losses from general funds and additional student fees. For example, University of Cincinnati subsidizes its sports programs to the tune of $15 million each year, on top of a $168.02 student fee per semester specifically for athletics.

Community colleges are experiencing the same trend. From 2004 to 2011, while overall community college instructional spending per student declined, athletic spending per athlete rose 35 percent.[15]

Let's sidestep the issue as to whether student athletes benefit from the current system. Despite a growing chorus claiming unpaid student athletes are exploited, football and basketball players at Division I schools do receive full scholarships. So let's give the status quo the benefit of the doubt and assume the vast majority do benefit. And with the recent O'Bannon ruling allowing cost-of-living stipends and trust fund payments of up to $5,000 per year, they'll benefit even more.

Then the current picture looks like this:

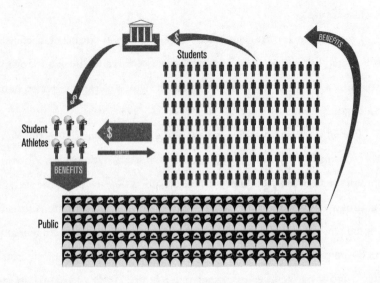

Dollars flow from tuition-paying students to student athletes while benefits flow to the public or back to the university in terms of prestige and increased enrollment. There are two ways that tuition-paying students benefit: increased school spirit and (potentially) enhanced value of their degree through enhanced prestige. (Although, truth be told, Oklahoma State alumni aren't feeling "enhanced" following *Sports Illustrated*'s 2013 five-part exposé on the rise of the school's football program.) But tuition-paying students are not capturing their fair share of benefits. Not even close. Which causes me to further question the already questionable adage from Rydell High's Principal McGee in the movie *Grease:* "If you can't be an athlete, be an athletic supporter."

Research

This all might be viewed as a curiosity (relegated to a particularly sweaty corner of higher education) if it weren't instructive for a larger and more important enterprise and the related governance question that arises: allocation of resources to research. For years, critics (mainly conservatives) have derided the research output of colleges and universities. Depending on the discipline, anywhere from 45 percent (sciences) to 98 percent (arts and humanities) of published research is never cited in any other publication. A 2009 report from the American Enterprise Institute pointed out that over the prior five years, the number of published language and literature articles had risen from 13,000 to 72,000.[16]

This outcome is predictable and highly formula-driven. Deanlets and department heads determine promotions and salary increases on quantity of publications (counting articles rather than reading them). And don't forget the damned college rankings—all of which include a measure of research productivity, and many of which are so research-weighted they're in danger of toppling over into irrelevance insofar as quality of undergraduate education is concerned.

These formulas ensure that teaching is subordinate to research at nearly all traditional colleges and universities, including community colleges. This is as true in the United Kingdom as it is in the United States. A new report from the UK's minister for universities estimates that for UK institutions established more than 50 years ago, 60 percent of total faculty time is allocated to research while only 40 percent is spent teaching students. "The pendulum has swung too far away from teaching," the report concludes, particularly when UK tuition has now increased to market levels (i.e., £9,000 per year). Back in the United States, a 2005 study in the *Journal of Higher Education* showed an inverse relationship between amount of time spent in the classroom and a faculty member's salary.[17] (And now that I've cited this study, its author assuredly will enjoy a raise and an even lower teaching load.)

Regardless, you don't have to be a critic of the research function to acknowledge that tuition-paying students, whose tuition dollars support a good amount of the research function, are not getting their fair share of the benefits. The comforting narrative of "faculty member at forefront of field imparting the state of the art to students in the classroom" aside (and at non-elite institutions, this narrative is fiction), the picture looks remarkably similar to the athletic one: Benefits flow primarily to the public and back to the university rather than to tuition-paying students.

How have trustees countenanced this trickery on tuition-paying students? Quite simply: Knowledge creation and dissemination is part of their mission. And few trustees are asking the hard questions.

AVOIDING THE COVER OF
BAD JUDGMENT MAGAZINE

Other than affordability, what should trustees focus on? Here are three ideas that could keep them off the cover of *Bad Judgment Magazine*.

1) Quality

As a rule, colleges and universities don't track whether students are learning. But when researchers have tried to dig in, what they've found is not encouraging. The Arum and Roksa study of 2,300 college graduates from two dozen universities found that a third of the students showed no improvement in critical thinking, analytical reasoning, or written communication.[18] In part, this is because students spend less time on school work than the prior generation: 10 fewer hours per week. About a third of students study less than 5 hours per week. On average, students spend 27 hours per week in study and class—roughly the same time commitment as kindergarten. Half of the seniors surveyed reported they did not write any papers longer than 20 pages.[19] Most courses don't assign more than 40 pages of reading per week.[20]

But it also may be that quality has declined. In early 2014, the College Educational Quality project was released. This was an in-depth look at two selective research institutions: one public, one private. A team from Columbia University's Teachers College spent a week in the spring of 2013 observing over 150 courses and scored academic rigor according to a strict rubric. Both universities scored 3.33 out of 5.5 for academic rigor and 2.97 out of 5.0 for teaching quality—scores that would get you a D in the classroom. And these were brand-name universities; few students can count on this level of instruction.

But this hasn't stopped colleges and universities from rewarding students for their work: 43 percent of all grades now given in higher education are A's (up from 33 percent 25 years ago). Unfortunately, few trustee meetings have academic rigor and teaching quality on the agenda.

2) Diversity

Fifty years ago, higher education was viewed as the great motor of American social mobility. Increasing evidence suggests not only that the motor has stalled, but that it may have shifted into reverse. Consider that:

- 75 percent of students at the 200 most selective colleges come from the top income quartile; only 5 percent come from the bottom quartile.[21]
- In the last decade, the percentage of students from families at the highest income levels who earned a bachelor's degree has grown to 82 percent while for students from the lowest income levels it has fallen to just 8 percent.[22]
- In the past 20 years, 80 percent of whites enrolled in higher education have attended top 500 schools while 75 percent of minority students have attended schools outside the top 500.[23]
- The gap in SAT scores between low-income and high-income students has widened about 40 percent in the past 40 years and is now double the gap between black and white students.[24]
- The share of students from the bottom income quartile at the 200 most selective colleges has been stuck at less than 5 percent for the past 20 years.[25]
- Only 41 percent of low-income students entering a four-year college managed to graduate within five years while 66 percent of high-income students did. This gap has been growing.[26]
- Only 22 percent of students at flagship universities receive Pell Grants compared to 35 percent across all colleges and universities. And among minority students, only 12 percent at flagship universities are Pell recipients compared to 24 percent across all institutions. The University of Virginia has a lower proportion of Pell recipients than Yale (11 vs. 13 percent).[27]

The statistics are damning: Colleges and universities are failing to live up to their end of the social bargain that got states into the business of funding higher education. According to Anthony Carnevale, director of

Georgetown's Center on Education and the Workforce, "Our postsecondary system has become highly segregated by class, by race and by ethnicity. It is more and more the case that the four-year college system is whiter and more affluent, [while] the two-year system is browner and blacker and more working class and some poor. In the end, the system is predictably reflecting the advantaged in the society."[28]

This problem stems directly from the unique level of heterogeneity across our colleges and universities, far outpacing that of any other country. Research over the past decade has demonstrated that state policies to sustain heterogeneous systems are increasing social inequality as students are matched to institutions based on their level of preparation. And heterogeneity is now receiving attention on a national level as a major source of the increase in inequality and decline in social and economic mobility. The 62 percent of Americans raised in the top 20 percent income bracket now remain in the top 40 percent for their entire lives, while the 65 percent raised in the bottom 20 percent income bracket remain in the bottom 40 percent.[29] So while we continue to have a merit-based system of higher education, "merit" in terms of income level is increasingly passed down from one generation to the next.

Elite institutions can and should be doing more. A study by William Bowen, former president of Princeton, found that, controlling for test scores, low-income students had no better chance of admission to 19 elite colleges than high-income students. Despite some recent measures taken by the very top schools (Harvard, Yale and Princeton shifted loans to grants), it's hard to imagine the top 5 percent of colleges unilaterally disarming in the rankings arms race by admitting large numbers of low-income students with lower SAT or ACT scores. Indeed, some colleges have climbed the rankings ladder over the past decade by doing just the opposite: reducing the percentage of low-income students. So, despite generous grant programs from our most elite institutions, it is as true as ever that diversity at top institutions means putting a rich kid from California in the same room as a rich kid from New York.

And even when it's a poor kid from California in the same room as a rich kid from New York, the culture at many institutions may actually be detrimental to the poor kid's social mobility. In their 2013 book *Paying for the Party: How College Maintains Inequality*, researchers tracked a group of female freshmen at an elite midwestern state institution. What they found was a fraternity and sorority-based "party pathway" that demands (and gives) little in terms of academics. The social pressure to "join the party" actually undercuts the social mobility and career aspirations of working class students. The working class students who fared best transferred from the state university to less prestigious schools.[30]

3) Technology

As with quality and diversity, college and university trustees aren't spending nearly enough time considering technology, let alone gaining expertise (outside of scheduled board meetings) as to how technology will transform higher education. With technology now the most potent "disruptor" to the current college business model, universities should be actively soliciting technology experts for their boards and adding experienced technology managers from outside higher education to their leadership teams—which is different from using technology as an excuse for administrative bloat. That's the only way they'll be able to turn technology from crisis to opportunity and keep their institutions off the cover of *Bad Judgment Magazine*.

FOUR

CRISIS OF DATA

IF YOU'VE SEEN OR READ MONEYBALL, THE STORY
of the unlikely success of baseball's out-of-the-box-thinking general manager, Billy Beane, you may have already drawn parallels to the current state
of higher education. Beane is the long-time GM of the Oakland Athletics,
a small-market team unable to keep up financially with richer competitors
and therefore in need of a differentiated strategy.

Early in *Moneyball* there's a scene of Billy sitting with his scouts, wise
old men of America's pastime, discussing which players to select in the
2002 draft. The scouts jaw on about players' arms, legs and bodies and
their potential. One scout insists that an ugly girlfriend means that a player
doesn't have confidence. The scouts are entranced by the obvious. When
it comes to metrics, the scouts focus on what's easy to measure. The scouts
love high school pitchers: "High school pitchers had brand-new arms, and
brand-new arms were able to generate the one asset scouts could measure:
a fastball's velocity."[1]

Moneyball's author Michael Lewis is an eager anthropologist observing
a new language. "The scouts use catchphrases to describe what they need

to avoid. "Rockhead" clearly isn't a good thing to be, but the quality can be overcome. "Soft" is also fairly damning—it connotes both "out of shape" and "wimp"—but it, too, is inconclusive. "'Bad makeup' is a death sentence. 'Bad makeup' means 'this kid's got problems we can't afford to solve.'"

At one point, Billy directs the discussion to Jeremy Brown, a catcher at the University of Alabama.

"Jeremy Brown is a bad-body catcher," says one of the old scouts.

"Let me ask you this," says Billy. "If Jeremy Brown looked as good in a uniform as Majewski [a University of Texas player with a great body and good face], where on this board would you put him?"

"He'd be in the first column. A first-round pick."

"You guys really are trying to sell jeans, aren't you?"

Early in his career with the A's, Beane recognized that the foundation of baseball management, seemingly solid, was perched precariously upon three cognitive errors: (1) the tendency to generalize wildly from one's own experience; (2) the tendency to be overly influenced by recent performance; and (3) the bias toward what you saw with your own eyes. While the first two are obviously problematic, the last one is less so, but more insidious for that very reason. As Lewis points out: "One absolutely cannot tell, by watching, the difference between a .300 hitter and a .275 hitter. The difference is one hit every two weeks . . . Certainly the average fan, seeing perhaps a tenth of the team's games, could never gauge two performances that accurately—in fact if you see both 15 games a year, there is a 40 percent chance that the .275 hitter will have more hits than the .300 hitter in the games that you see. The difference between a good hitter and an average hitter is simply not visible—it is a matter of record."

Billy Beane was very clear: The Oakland A's could not allow themselves to be victimized by what they saw. Like other small-market teams, they didn't have the luxury. They had to begin doing things differently. So

Billy brought data to the table in the form of Paul DePodesta, a Harvard graduate with an economics degree and a statistics-spewing laptop ready at hand.

It turns out that pitchers who haven't attended college are much less likely to have successful major league careers than comparable pitchers who have attended college. And when you try to correlate certain statistics to runs scored, batting average is a poor indicator, but on base percentage (OBP) is highly correlated. So Beane and the A's decided to eschew high school pitchers and focus on OBP; the A's began to value and acquire players with a knack for getting on base any way they can, especially by taking walks (or, painfully, getting hit by a pitch).

The most amazing result of all of this is not that the A's unlikely group of major leaguers won 20 games in a row—still a record—and made the playoffs in 2002, the season chronicled in *Moneyball*. It is this: If gross miscalculations of a person's value can occur on a baseball field, before a live audience of 30,000 and a television audience of millions more, what does that say about the measurement of performance in other lines of work?

"My only question is if he's that good a hitter, why doesn't he hit better?"

—Billy Beane

Beane was only able to do what he did with the A's because 20 years earlier a man named Bill James began a protest movement in the form of a photocopied, stapled 68-page booklet mailed to 75 people.

James is famous for having done two things. First, he revolutionized how we think about data in baseball. For example, walks had historically been viewed as a mistake by the pitcher. In early box scores, walks were recorded as an error. That view continues to pervade baseball to this day, as evidenced by the fact that a walk is not counted as an at-bat, and therefore no statistical credit is given to the hitter despite the fact that walks can constitute as much as half of OBP.

Second, James realized we'd never get to the promised land of rational, data-driven management without the right data. Fielding is a good example. Before James and Beane came along, the only statistic kept for fielding was errors. What's an error? An error is an obvious mistake by a fielder who gets to the ball in time and then fails to catch or throw it correctly. But the statistic not only gives no credit to the fielder who gets to the ball in time, it penalizes him. So James proposed a new statistic—the "range factor." A player's range factor was simply the number of successful plays he made in the field per game.

Baseball teams didn't know what to collect and so a lot of critical data went unrecorded: the pitch count at the end of at bats, how batters performed in different counts and game situations, pitch types and locations, who was pitching when a base was stolen, the direction and distance of batted balls and where exactly they landed, how many pitches a pitcher threw in a game.

So in the early 1980s, James proposed to take the collection of statistics out of the hands of baseball teams and build an organization of volunteer scorekeepers who would collect the necessary data. The movement was called sabermetrics, after SABR, the Society for American Baseball Research. One James disciple did exactly this, establishing a company called STATS Inc. James joined as an investor and creative director. After five years of trying and failing to convince baseball teams to pay for this new data, STATS Inc. began selling the data to fans. The fans understood the importance of the data ten years before the year of *Moneyball*.

Why did the revolution take so long? Because baseball was run by insiders—men who had played the game and subscribed to all three cognitive errors. Billy, too, was a former ballplayer. But he was able to see through the illusions because he himself had been one.

Around the time that Bill James was getting started, Billy Beane had "a body you could dream on. Ramrod-straight and lean . . . And that face! . . . Billy had the Good Face." Every scout who saw him fervently believed Billy was the second coming. Except he wasn't. When it came time to step into the batter's box, something happened. He doubted himself. He got angry and broke a lot of equipment. The numbers spoke for themselves. After a decade, he'd hit .219 in only 301 at-bats in Major League Baseball. The rest of the time he rode the bench, or the bus for minor league clubs. But the worst part for Billy—the only thing he really regretted—was that out of high school he took a $125,000 signing bonus to join the New York Mets organization and gave up a scholarship to Stanford.

MONEY COLLEGE

"A young player is not what he looks like, or what he might become, but what he has done."

—Billy Beane

If Billy had gone to Stanford, he might have helped instigate higher education's own data-driven revolution. To paraphrase Beane, a college is not what it looks like, or what the rankings say, but what it has done. But its measurements of performance are much worse than baseball statistics before James and Beane. Higher education remains a line of work where the measurements of performance are fundamentally broken.

For baseball it may have been body parts, batting average and the number on the radar gun. For higher education, it's the four Rs. Each of these areas is easily quantified or judged: research citations or number of publications in *Nature* and *Science*; how much has been spent on a new building and how stately, innovative and generally impressive it appears; BCS (college football Bowl Championship Series) standings; and *U.S. News* rankings, or take your pick from among a plethora of hungry new rankings, so prevalent that *Times Higher Education,* the authoritative source for higher education news in the UK, now devotes an entire section to new whiz-bang ranking systems.

Unfortunately, the four Rs correlate about as closely to student outcomes and return on investment as batting average or fastball velocity, which is to say, not at all. Take rankings, for example. One's position in the Shanghai Jiao Tong University rankings—the best known global university rankings—is the "ugly girlfriend" of higher education. In fact, studies have shown that the year-to-year variability among institutions in rankings is greater than could be plausibly attributed to actual changes in institutional quality.

As Paul Lingenfelter of the State Higher Education Executive Officers noted, "Our fundamental problem is that we don't have very good ways of measuring our fundamental product . . . the key is getting some agreement about learning outcomes and . . . generating more of them."[2] And so, like Bill James in the late 1970s, we are in need of new data to help us understand which institutions, programs and modes of delivery produce the best outcomes in terms of student learning and employment.

The good news is that we can't do much worse. Famously, the Department of Education's Integrated Postsecondary Education Data System (IPEDS) only tracks persistence and graduation rates for first-time, full-time freshmen, thereby omitting the majority of students who are transfers or part-time students. According to Stan Jones, president of Complete College America, "We know they enroll, but we don't know what happens to them. We shouldn't make policy based on the image of students going straight from high school to college, living on campus, and graduating four years later, when the majority of college students don't do that."[3] Last year, in an admission of the problem, the Department of Education announced that it intends to include part-time and transfer students in graduation rates. But there is no timetable for accomplishing this.

Significantly, there currently is absolutely no outcome data related to student learning. We know what courses students have taken and their grades. But we don't know what students are supposed to have learned in these courses, what capabilities they are supposed to be able to demonstrate as a result, and the extent to which they've done so. All of this is as mysterious as religion. In an age of terabytes of data, it's shocking. It's no wonder that dystopian doubt has crept in.

There are a number of reasons why we lack this data. The primary one, however, is that because payments for higher education are made for inputs rather than for outputs, no one has bothered to collect and report it. Students enroll and pay tuition in order to receive 45 hours of seat time for a three-credit course (as well as 90 additional hours of reading and work outside the classroom). That's what universities are paid for. That's what they deliver.

The ultimate task is Sisyphean: tracking students years and decades after exiting colleges and universities—a level of complexity several orders of magnitude greater than tracking every aspect of 2,500 baseball games each year. A report issued last year by the National Research Council (NRC) adopted a melancholy tone: "While productivity measurement in many service sectors is fraught with conceptual and data difficulties, nowhere are the challenges—such as accounting for input differences, wide quality variation of outputs, and opaque or regulated pricing—more imposing than for higher education."[4]

This is the battle over the so-called unit record system. Everyone wants it, except when they think about the privacy concerns such a system would elicit. Nevertheless, the NRC report supports such a system and both the Bush and Obama administrations have pursued it with varying degrees of intensity. The obstacle: objections in Congress driven by lobbyists for colleges concerned about what such a system would reveal. These objections culminated in the Higher Education Act specifically forbidding the creation of a federal unit record database. Republicans tend to lead the charge here, linking a comprehensive system to the implementation of No-Child-Left-Behind-style federal command-and-control in higher education.

In response, the Obama administration has offered states funding to construct their own longitudinal databases. Tennessee is farthest ahead, having designed a funding formula based on 13 outcomes metrics. The Illinois Board of Higher Education has formed a working group from state government, higher education and business to design metrics to be used to evaluate university performance. Mississippi, Texas, Colorado and Arkansas aren't far behind. Even California has developed a tool that evaluates community colleges based on completion of any postsecondary credential within six years. Many states now have such a system in progress, although they'll miss the many students who traverse state lines to complete college.

Driven by these efforts and an alphabet soup of higher education associations, Congress is now back for another try at a federal system. The amended Student Right to Know Before You Go Act, sponsored by Senators Marco Rubio (R-FL), Ron Wyden (D-OR) and Mark Warner (D-VA) includes a federal unit record system. The system would link with Social Security and other databases to accurately track graduates' wages. The bill stands little chance of passing. A less ambitious bill—the Investigating Postsecondary Education Data for Students Act, which simply directs a federal committee to study what new data is required—has passed the house, effectively sidelining Know Before You Go.

In the absence of governmental leadership, private organizations are stepping up. The National Student Clearinghouse is a not-for-profit association that collects data from 3,300 colleges and universities and made a big splash in 2013 by announcing our national completion rate: 54 percent. Still, the Clearinghouse is limited in that its agreements with colleges prohibit releasing anything other than aggregated data that does not identify the institution. Even the NRC panel emphasized it was important to avoid institution-by-institution comparisons for fear of incentivizing institutions to lower graduation requirements.

Based on National Student Clearinghouse data, the Gates Foundation has funded a group of six major higher education organizations to develop new measures of student success. Not surprisingly, the only institutions that will identify themselves as part of this project are those that look worse under the current metrics, e.g., the University of Southern Indiana where 30 percent of graduates are transfer students. Others are continuing to work the problem. The Lumina Foundation is working with the American Institutes for Research and six states with the hope of releasing graduates' starting salary data by institution and program. No target date has been set for this ambitious effort.

The most valuable contribution to date is the Voluntary Institutional Metrics Project, another Gates-backed initiative. For this project, 18 institutions banded together to create new sources of data in five areas, including student learning, student progression and completion, and employment, and to do so in a way that doesn't simply measure outputs, but correlates them to the caliber of inputs. So, instead of simply showing an institution's output on a given measure, it compares that output against a predicted range based on inputs such as percentage of Pell students.

It's understandable why people get discouraged by the magnitude of the effort required and the lack of progress to date. Assuming a national unit record system is still years away, once we have accurate completion data on an institution basis, we'll have taken only the first step. For that statistic won't be representative for all students. For example, female students will probably perform better than males. Students coming straight from high school or in their 30s perform better than students in their early 20s. Students who take honors courses will do better than students who take remedial courses.

Still, continuing to focus on the four Rs in the wake of the seismic shifts underway in higher education is equivalent to the baseball fan staggering out of the stadium after a night game and searching for his car keys. Where does he look for them? Not where he lost them, but under the light because that's where he can see. Only one thing is clear here: He's not driving home. (And by the way, he should stop looking, because driving in his condition is dangerous!)

The problem with higher education is that, unlike baseball, there is no objective measure of success like wins or World Series championships. Rankings are accepted as the best proxy, and it would be professional suicide for a president to take her institution in a very different direction.

SIGNAL METRICS

"Bozdee bozdee bop. Didy bop."
—David Lee Roth, "Just a Gigolo"

On an institutional level, university presidents don't have the data they need to manage effectively. Universities are complex and difficult organizations to manage in large part because there are no clear, agreed-upon metrics to determine whether there is a problem—for example, are students actually learning?

A similarly complex situation arose in the early 1980s as video began killing the radio star. Back then, the paradigm of male licentiousness was Van Halen's lead singer David Lee Roth. Known for his spandex pants, mesh tops and scarves, heavy eyeliner and long, flowing blond hair, Roth combined the fashion sense of glam rock with the aggressive heterosexuality of heavy metal. But parents could care less about antecedents. To them, David Lee Roth was "Runnin' with the Devil."

Concert promoters thought the same thing, but for a very different reason. When a promoter sought to book Van Halen for a show, Van Halen provided the promoter with a contract rider outlining the promoter's responsibilities. According to Roth, "most rock and roll bands had a contract rider like a pamphlet. We had one that was like the Chinese phone book."[5] While staging concerts for other bands might have been as easy as "Dancing in the Street," Van Halen concerts were more of a "Mean Street."

Right in the middle of the Van Halen rider was a stipulation that while M&Ms must be provided for the enjoyment of the band and crew, there were to be no brown M&Ms backstage. If any brown M&Ms were found, the promoter would be in breach and the band would get paid without having to play.

Word got out about the Van Halen brown M&M clause, and for years it represented the apex of rock excess: forcing someone to search through M&Ms and remove the brown ones. The clause is parodied in the 1984 film *This Is Spinal Tap* when guitarist Nigel Tufnel complains to his manager about his inability to fit normal size cold cuts on miniature bread: "But then if you keep folding it, it keeps breaking. And then everything has to be folded, and then it's this. And I don't want this. I want large bread."

But the brown M&M provision is actually as interesting as it is amusing. Van Halen's show was bigger and more complex than any previous arena production. Roth was playing some very old buildings with a range of technical issues: insufficient voltage or amperage, inability to accommodate the 850 par lamp lights Van Halen needed for its show, load bearing restrictions on stage.

Roth explained the true story in a 2012 interview:

If I came backstage and I saw brown M&Ms on the catering table, it guaranteed the promoter had not read the contract rider, and we had to do a serious check. Because frequently we had danger issues . . . Well, after seeing brown M&Ms and ceremoniously and very theatrically destroying the dressing room to try to get the message across lest we have a disaster . . . the word got around, "hey, take this seriously."[6]

The brown M&M provision was the perfect solution to the complex situation Van Halen faced as it was playing new venues: an easily discernible metric that effectively signals whether there is a problem. If David Lee Roth had less musical talent and better taste in apparel, this son of a very wealthy eye surgeon might have been a university president. A President Roth would develop a similar metric for his institution. And given the technical wizardry of Van Halen shows, technology would be key. Because what kind of signal metric is available to universities without technology? Taking attendance? Weekly quizzes? No student wants to be treated like a third-grader. As we'll see in the next chapter, technology will go a long way to solving the Crisis of Data for colleges and universities, allowing forward-thinking presidents (like the David Lee Roth of my imagination), to create signal metrics that will allow them to do a much better job of running their institutions.

MAKING RESEARCH PAY

Although I've denigrated research as disconnected from student outcomes, there's an important opportunity for one of the four Rs to redeem itself. Few faculty members in education, economics, statistics and applied mathematics have turned their research expertise and resources on their own institutions.

It's estimated that less than $1 billion is spent in the United States each year on education research, with the federal government spending about $700 million and universities, foundations and the private sector spending about $300 million.[7] To put this in context, consider that medicine and education should be two sides of the same coin. In developed democracies, both are services to which all citizens are entitled regardless of birth, station or resources. Medicine advances human health and happiness. Education advances economic productivity and happiness. Then consider that $140 billion is spent in the United States each year on medical research.[8] In context, $1 billion on education research is peanuts.

How to explain the 140:1 ratio? Medicine may well be more important than education, but it's not 140 times more important. One answer is that medical research is easier: Health typically can be directly measured and quantified; education cannot. Education can only be measured derivatively. Derivative measurement adds a degree of subjectivity and difficulty to the question of whether learning has occurred. No such equivocation is possible when the question is discrete and relatively straightforward to investigate with control groups—for example, whether a weight loss regimen has been effective, or whether a new drug lowers cholesterol levels.

The other reason is related but distinct: There are clear and willing payers for improved medical outcomes. Employers and the government fund insurance plans that cover proven treatments. Innovation in medicine is amply rewarded as better outcomes are met with fistfuls of private or government insurance dollars. In contrast, while employers obviously prefer an adequately educated workforce (in addition to a healthy workforce), there are no insurers offering to cover the costs of remediation.

Employers struggle and there is no such thing as education insurance because education is harder to measure. So there is no clear definition of a "proven treatment" or an "educational standard of care."

If medical research far outpaced education research over the past century, look for education research to at least keep up over the next hundred years. The reason: big data.

Big data will make education much easier to measure and make education research more like medical research. Think about the challenge posed by Ken Koedinger of Carnegie Mellon in a recent *New York Times Magazine* article: "To maximize retention of information, it's best to start out by exposing the student to the information at short intervals, gradually lengthening the amount of time between encounters." But different types of information require different schedules of exposure that need to be adjusted according to each student's mastery, so "there's no way a classroom teacher can keep track of all this for every kid."[9]

While a classroom teacher or a researcher seeking to investigate this pacing issue in an on-ground environment won't make much progress, online delivery can produce terabytes of data that could provide the best answers for every learning objective.

Or, consider the question of whether learning can be improved through instructor gesturing, facial expressions, and eye gaze—also impossible to measure in a classroom, but possible through pedagogical agents or avatars in online classrooms producing terabytes of data for analysis. The more data, the more effective the learning will be, particularly for emerging learning systems.

A ton of educational innovations are coming down the pike as a result of big data that will turn "learning"—heretofore somewhat ineffable—into a science replete with clear definitions, standards and replicable studies that advance our knowledge of what produces the best outcomes and the best signal metrics. To future generations, education will seem a lot closer to medicine than it does today. And this should help attract talented professionals into education research and practice.

One implication of emerging technologies for delivering higher education—the subject of the next chapter—is that this work needs to become an institutional priority at research universities. When it does, hundreds of educational Bill Jameses will uncover important new variables and correlations and establish new outcomes-based rankings that, in time, will supplant the legacy input-based systems.

If colleges (and college players) can provide the data necessary for the data revolution in baseball, they can certainly do so for the revolution at home. It will result in dozens of would-be Billy Beanes springing up across the country—particularly at small colleges and universities, the higher education equivalent of the "small market Oakland A's"—arguing what the on-base percentage equivalent for higher education is, coalescing around signal metrics that are meaningful for all students, and helping their institutions reform and restructure to increase "wins."

FIVE

FINDING WONDERLAND

IN THE SUMMER OF 2012, THE TWIN QUASARS OF the *New York Times* opinion page—Thomas Friedman and David Brooks—waxed poetic about the coming revolution in higher education. Elite universities were moving online with "MOOCs" (massive open, online courses): MIT and Harvard with edX; Stanford, Princeton, Penn and Michigan with Coursera. Friedman wrote, "In five years, this will be a huge industry."[1]

The twin quasars were right about the revolution, but wrong about the vehicle. Still, the story of MOOCs—the biggest higher education story of the decade—provides a fascinating window on how technology will change higher education.

In January 2012, Sebastian Thrun, an adjunct professor of computer science at Stanford, invited the world to attend his fall semester artificial intelligence course. To the annoyance of Stanford officials, he ended up with 160,000 online students. Thrun then announced he would stop teaching at Stanford and direct all his teaching activities through Udacity, a startup that would offer online courses from leading professors to millions of students. Professor Thrun called the experience of reaching so many students life changing: "Having done this, I can't teach at Stanford again. I feel there's a red pill and a blue pill. And you can take the blue pill and go back to your classroom and lecture your 20 students. But I've taken the red pill, and I've seen Wonderland."[2]

As soon as I watched Thrun's talk, I had the funny sense I'd seen this movie before. Take a look at this excerpt from a dot-com era *New York Times* article with the headline "Boola, E-Commerce Comes to The Quad," which anticipated Professor Thrun's announcement by 12 years:

> Distance learning sells the knowledge inside a professor's head directly to a global online audience. That means that, just by doing what he does every day, a teacher potentially could grow rich instructing a class consisting of a million students signed up by the Internet-based educational firm that marketed the course and handles the payments. "Faculty are dreaming of returns that are probably multiples of their lifetime net worth," said Kim Clark, dean of the Harvard Business School. "They are doing things like saying, 'This technology allows someone who is used to teaching 100 students to teach a million students.' And they are running numbers and imagining, 'Gee, what if everyone paid $10 to listen to my lecture?'"[3]

The turn of the millennium was a heady time, and many in higher education really believed the hype that brand-name institutions would grow to hundreds of thousands of students and that "rock star" faculty would get rich teaching millions of students online. But today the only universities with hundreds of thousands of students are for-profit universities invented in the past 30 years, and the only educator who has become a rock star through the Internet is in K-to-12, not higher education (more on him in a moment).

So what happened? Higher education commentator Kevin Carey described Thrun's first MOOC at Stanford: "Over 100,000 students around the world [took] the course . . . Those who did well got a certificate from the professor saying so."[4]

But Stanford's official response to Carey's description was as follows: "Students who did well did not receive a certificate. Neither Stanford nor the professors issued a certificate. All students who completed the courses received a letter from the professor saying that they had completed the course. And that's it."[5]

Hell may freeze over before Stanford is willing to provide any meaningful credential for MOOCs. That's a problem, because employers continue to love degrees—a convenient and conventional signal that a candidate is worthy of consideration. For many jobs, hiring managers could lose their jobs if they dared to hire someone without a degree. And although the income gap between college graduates and the hoi polloi may be lower than conventionally thought, there's no question that the gap exists and remains the primary motivation for enrollment. (If love of learning were the beating heart of the higher education industry, we would live in a better world. But it isn't. And we don't.)

What the turn-of-the-millennium rock-star-logic missed, and what its MOOC-sequel also missed, is that the online learning experience from the rock star faculty member from the brand-name university must lead to a credential value-bearing in the labor market.

Unfortunately for everyone—students, employers and the twin quasars alike—the gap between exclusive residential degree programs for 18-to-22-year-olds and online learning open to everyone is a chasm that no institution has crossed. Putting content and individual courses online is fine for elite institutions. But issuing credits, let alone credentials, is an existential threat. You can almost hear the whispering through the Ivy: "If this online program leads to a Princeton degree, what does that say about the degree programs we offer on campus?" MIT tried to be cute here, creating MITx as a separate organization that might have granted MITx credentials. But then Harvard joined up, made MIT change the name to edX, and—in typical Harvard fashion—ruined everything.

THE SPICE GIRLS OF HIGHER EDUCATION

MOOCs were supposed to create rock stars, but in music parlance they're a flash in the pan. Consider this:

- Completion rates appear to be less than 5 percent (although if you use the number of students completing the first assignment as the denominator—a statistical leap with a degree of difficulty bordering on incredulous—it may be as high as 40 percent).
- 80 percent of enrolled students already have degrees.
- 80 percent of enrolled students are from outside the United States.
- Overall traffic to MOOCs is falling rapidly despite increasing course offerings—meaning enrollments per course are plummeting; the days of the six-figure enrollment MOOC are long gone.

It is thus that MOOCs became the Spice Girls of higher education. There are a number of similarities. To wit:

Fact #1: Instant global phenomena
Both the Spice Girls and MOOCs were instant global phenomena. Over the course of a few weeks in the fall/winter of 1996/97, with "Wannabe" climbing the charts to #1 in 31 countries, the Spice Girls became the fastest selling British act since the Beatles. All

they needed to do to attract a crowd was show up, e.g., 500,000 people turned out to watch them turn on the Christmas lights in Oxford Street. For MOOCs, that period was the fall/winter of 2011/12, following the Stanford (Thrun/Norvig) MOOC on artificial intelligence that enrolled 160,000 students, and the subsequent creation of Udacity and Coursera, which founder Andrew Ng boasted was "growing faster than Facebook."[6]

Fact #2: Role of the media

Both the Spice Girls and MOOCs were media-driven phenomena. Their catchy monikers—Posh Spice, Ginger Spice, Scary Spice, Sporty Spice and Baby Spice—were a creation of *Top of the Pops* magazine. Newspapers picked up the names and suddenly they were the most widely recognized group of individuals since John, Paul, George and Ringo. MOOC is also a catchy name. Although not invented by the media, the media popularized and covered it with greater intensity than any higher education story in memory. The *New York Times* called 2012 "The Year of the MOOC." For many casual observers, MOOC became synonymous with higher education.

Fact #3: Seemed different, but really more of the same

When the Spice Girls came on the scene, they seemed fresh and different. We'd never heard anything like this before:

> *I'll tell you what I want, what I really really want,*
>
> *. . .*
>
> *I wanna, I wanna, I wanna, I wanna, I wanna really*
> *really really wanna zigazig ha!*

I want to make two points here. First, by quoting "zigazig ha!" I really, really may have achieved my purpose here on earth. Second, although they seemed different, the Spice Girls were really just a boy band in a different form. The Spice Girls origins story begins with a talent management company placing an ad in a trade magazine that sought to recruit an all-girl band. According to one of the managers, the objective was to take the boy band formula—which appealed fairly exclusively to girls—and create an all-girl band that would appeal to boys as well. So the Spice Girls should be viewed as firmly part of a proud lineage tracing back to Backstreet Boys and NSYNC, and continuing to One Direction.

Similarly, universities in the dot-com era endeavored to project their content or teaching to large audiences: beginning with Fathom (Columbia, LSE, Chicago, Michigan) and the Princeton-Oxford-Stanford-Yale initiatives, which posted lectures and short Webinars online, and continuing with MIT OpenCourseWare, through which MIT posted all course materials for public consumption. The 2011–2013 era MOOCs added a few elements, but nothing that could be called revolutionary. In fact, in a 2014 interview, Sebastian Thrun said that he had finally found the magic formula. What was it? Thrun's magic formula was not a fully automated online class featuring prerecorded videos and Web-based assessments. In other words, it wasn't a MOOC at all. To get better results, he said, "We changed the equation and put people on the ground." By adding mentors and a help line, and making phone calls to remind students to do their work, Udacity found it could get more students to do the work, finish the course and pass. Longer term, he has some ideas about using adaptive learning software to eliminate some of this labor, but for now it takes manpower.[7]

The magic formula sounds uncannily like the online degree programs already offered by hundreds of accredited higher education institutions in which over three million American students are currently enrolled.

Fact #4: Still represented something important

Nevertheless, both the Spice Girls and MOOCs represented something much more important than themselves. When Ginger Spice wore her Union Jack dress at the 1997 Brit Awards, it became the global image of Cool Britannia, the movement and social climate that emerged along with the election of Tony Blair and New Labor in the spring of 1997. MOOCs represented the moment when all of higher education—including our most prestigious institutions—not only began to take online learning seriously, but embraced it as central to the future. Suddenly, not having an online strategy was not an option. Trustees began to raise the question at every board meeting. Presidents who failed to come up with an appropriate answer (or even a stalling tactic) might find their jobs on the line.

Overall, MOOCs had it half right with the final "OC": online course. The first half, "MO," is a mistake. Making courses massive and open make them less appealing to students. And, as we shall see, online courses needn't be massive or open to be incredibly useful and affordable.

A major event in the downfall of MOOCs was the pilot with San Jose State University. In January 2013, Thrun was applauded when he announced that Udacity would pilot remedial and introductory MOOCs with San Jose State and offer them for credit. Thrun said he hoped the $150 price point would change higher education, while California Governor Jerry Brown said: "Whatever it costs, it'll be cheaper than a high-speed rail."[8]

Thrun and Brown were correct in highlighting the effort's importance. While over three million students are pursuing a degree program from a US college or university entirely online, without ever setting foot on campus, online learning has really only addressed the first of the three major challenges it ought to help solve.

Continuing the work of the private sector universities that put campuses at highway interchanges and in shopping malls, online learning has made college accessible to every American adult with an Internet connection. But Thrun and Brown were looking forward to stage 2 and stage 3 of the online revolution.

As the state of California is still the single largest funding source of the University of California and California State (CSU) systems, Brown was enthusiastic about the potential to lower costs. After all, online learning hadn't yet made an impact on affordability; kowtowing to price as a signal of quality in higher education, only a handful of institutions that had ventured online had dared price their online programs below the same on-ground programs, without regard to the actual (typically much lower) cost of online delivery.

For his part, Thrun was excited about helping CSU teach better; 50 percent of entering San Jose State (SJSU) students cannot meet basic requirements, and "cannot pass our elementary math and English placement tests," said Provost Ellen Junn.[9] And Thrun was determined to demonstrate that online delivery could be better than on-ground classes. While virtually every study on the question demonstrated that online delivery was as effective as traditional classroom delivery, none of these studies randomly assigned students to classroom or online delivery. So what they actually showed is that students who are inclined to select an online program perform as well or better than students who are not so inclined. Thrun wanted to show that online learning's potential wasn't rooted in self-selection.

A noble effort, but Thrun and SJSU did not see the irony of the MOOC—a medium with a course completion rate of 5 percent—as a solution for students who typically complete degrees at a rate of less than 25 percent. Naturally, the results were disappointing: course pass rates between 23.8 and 50.5 percent, well below comparable SJSU courses.[10] By the end of 2013, a year that had started so promisingly, SJSU and Udacity had parted ways.

And so the billion-dollar question in higher education—how to use technology to build fundamental skills (remedial education) and grant a credential of value at the end—remains unanswered. But I'm sure of two things: It will be answered in the next five years, and the answer won't simply use technology to faithfully replicate the traditional on-ground experience, but instead will take advantage of technology to provide a better experience.

Think of Apple's iPhone in contrast to prior phones. Steve Jobs and Jony Ive designed the iPhone not so that it would be familiar to early Nokia smartphone or Blackberry users, but rather by rethinking what a smartphone could be. And they took advantage of current technology to do it better.

Those seeking to use technology to improve education might get lucky by looking at an unexpected source: the gambling industry.

SLOTS OF FUN

I had the pleasure of attending law school in New Haven right after legalized gambling was introduced to puritan New England in the form of the giant Foxwoods Casino in nearby Ledyard, Connecticut. During my first year I attended the opening of the rival Mohegan Sun and remember thinking how fortunate I was to attend a law school that graded on a pass/fail basis.

But I didn't take advantage of the situation as much as my brother and my other roommate. Many Friday afternoons I'd return home to a note that read "Gone to Foxwoods" or sometimes just "Foxwoods" (if they were in a real hurry). They were perfect gambling partners. My brother Aaron was fairly impulsive, prone to making bets he shouldn't make, and appearing shocked and stunned every time they didn't pan out. My roommate Dave—the instigator but a conservative Yankee at heart—would badger my brother into leaving and then provide consolation as it dawned on both of them that my brother would complete law school with significantly more student loan debt than budgeted.

Their game was blackjack. They'd spend five to six hours at a table without taking a break. They'd typically return at 3 or 4 a.m., wake me up, and regale me with tales of doubling down, splitting and then splitting again, and ultimately some brush with a dealer or pit boss that—so the story went—had earned them the ire of the entire Pequot nation.

They were never much for slots, bypassing them every time on their way to the table games, dismissing them as entertainment for senior citizens. I'm not so sure they'd do the same today. On a recent visit to Las Vegas, I was amazed at the transformation of the slot machine. What I remember as a single genus of one-armed bandits, most with bars, cherries and lemons, has evolved into species that look, feel and sound markedly distinct from one another.

Today, these machines are by far the busiest and most popular games at casinos, and generate seven of every ten gambling dollars. Slots and other video machines are the game of choice for 90 percent of Gamblers Anonymous attendees in Las Vegas. And slots aren't just for seniors anymore. Among gamblers ages 36 to 50, 73 percent play slots while only 15 percent play table games. For 21-to-35-year-olds, 69 percent play slot machines and 18 percent play table games. Every day, Americans pump more than $1 billion into slot machines.[11]

What's changed? It's not just that there are more slot machines. On my first visit to Las Vegas in 1989, my father booked us a room at the Aladdin—an aging hotel-casino with acres of torn-up red carpets that seemed to be waiting for a new era. Indeed, Steve Wynn had just opened the Mirage across the street. But the Aladdin's casino floor was already crammed with slot machines.

Nearly a quarter century, a tiger mauling and a dozen Cirque du Soleil shows later, it's clearly not just about accessibility (although there are now 850,000 machines in the United States, twice as many as ATMs). It's about how technology and research have made slot machines more effective at parting gamblers from their money.

In 1976 the digital-video slot machine was born, ushering in an era of simplistic, immersive and distraction-free gambling. Why does digital technology have such an impact? By establishing a relationship with the player that exploits our psychological traits. Natasha Dow Schull of MIT describes this as an "embodied relation" by which a gambling machine becomes an extension of the gambler's own cognitive capacities and spatial skills.[12]

According to a recent paper in the *Journal of Gambling Studies,* the digital hooks are as follows:

1. The illusion of control: pressing buttons to produce the outcome.
2. Appearing to operate on a variable payout: fooling the player into thinking that the more they play, the more likely they are to win.
3. The near-miss: games programmed to tease players with near-misses about 30 percent of the time. And, according to research, a near-miss provides almost the same high as a win.
4. Increased arousal: bells and whistles matter.
5. Immediate gratification: perhaps most important. There is no waiting for another person, no interruptions—speed means more bets, and that means more excitement.[13]

Despite the fact that slots provide the worst odds in the casino—or, at least tied at the bottom with keno—gamblers increasingly flock to slots to lose money. You'd think they would learn. Perhaps by applying the lessons of slot machines, in a few years they'll be able to do just that.

The traditional classroom is like a blackjack table. You must visit the facility in order to participate. Sessions start when the leader says so. There are complex rules of participation. The session proceeds in a manner that is not individually tailored to your preferences. And sticking with it requires a focus on the long-term goal (i.e., earning a degree, or winning back your money).

It's understandable where MOOC mania came from: a thirst for something more than what's offered in run-of-the-mill courses. Online learning changed some of these elements. You no longer need to visit a campus. Sessions start much more frequently. But the harder parts (complex rules, not individually tailored, long-term focus) remained constant. It's the equivalent of 1989 at the Aladdin, replete with torn-up red carpets: on The Strip and accessible, but far from achieving its potential.

So the path for the next few years is clear. As in gambling, technology is important in higher education for increasing access, but more so because it enables several developments that will make learning much more affordable and effective (and perhaps addictive).

1. COMPETENCY-BASED LEARNING AND SIMPLICITY

For me, the most important pearl of wisdom to come out of the rise and fall of MOOCs was also referenced in Thrun's "Wonderland" speech:

> We really set up our students for failure. We don't help students to become smart. I started realizing that grades are the failure of the education system. [When students don't earn good grades, it means] educators have failed to bring students to A+ levels. So rather than grading students, my task was to make students successful. So it couldn't be about harsh, difficult questions. We changed the course so the questions were still hard, but students could attempt them multiple times. And when they finally got them right, they would get their A+. And it was much better. That really made me think about the education system as a whole. Salman Khan has this wonderful story. When you learn to ride a bicycle, and you fail to learn to ride a bicycle, you don't stop learning to ride the bicycle, give the person

a D, and then move on to a unicycle. You keep training them as long as it takes. And then they can ride a bicycle. Today, when someone fails, we don't take time to make them a strong student. We give them a C or a D, move them to the next class. Then they're branded a loser, and they're set up for failure. This medium has the potential to change all that.

In citing Salman Khan, founder of Khan Academy, Thrun referenced the first (and still only) rock star of online education. If you haven't had the pleasure of watching a Khan video, you haven't missed much in the way of the simulations, animations and expensive special effects many dot-com pundits predicted would dominate online learning. A Khan video is short, just a few minutes, and teaches a single concept. It does so by showing Khan's hand on the whiteboard while you hear his narration—an approach that is especially effective for math.

Khan is a rock star because the fireworks in his videos are pedagogical, not technological. Students are meant to take as much time as they need to master the concept in each video, which is revolutionary. Think about it: All education—not just higher education—is still organized according to a calendar that was developed to serve an agrarian economy: home over the summer to help with the crops. Each level of education is broken into years, and each year into terms. In order to progress from term to term or year to year, the student must demonstrate mastery of the subject within the requisite period. Failure simply means the student did not demonstrate mastery in time.

In a decade, online education may be recognized not for making higher education accessible to anyone with a smartphone, but rather as the midwife who delivered competency-based learning into the world. While competency-based learning is theoretically possible in a non-technology-enabled environment, it's not nearly as simple and appealing.

Online competency-based learning has the following characteristics, in this order:

- Curriculum that begins with competencies—defined in association with employers (who are expected to hire graduates) at the program and course levels. Note: while "competencies" is a term often viewed as synonymous with job-related skills, it should be interpreted as "capabilities," including cognitive capabilities, such as problem solving, numerical reasoning and locating information, as well as behavioral characteristics such as teamwork and accepting feedback.
- Course- or unit-level summative assessments that demonstrate mastery of the defined competencies.
- Course- or unit-level curricula that equip students with the defined competencies and prepare students to demonstrate them on the summative assessments.

Starting with competencies, then building assessments and only then developing curricula is a more logical way to educate than the seat-time model, that starts with curricula, then derives learning outcomes from the curricula, and then develops assessments.

Done properly, competency-based learning reduces the cost of delivery by half over standard online delivery. Equally important, competency-based learning improves efficacy by replacing a highly complex system—in which students must demonstrate mastery in an arbitrary period of time in order to progress—with simplicity, which is more important than you might think.

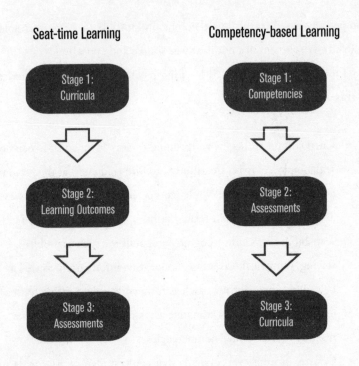

SIMPLE IS AS SIMPLE DOES

It is far more difficult to be simple than to be complicated; far more difficult to sacrifice skill and easy execution in the proper place than to expand both indiscriminately.

—John Ruskin, Victorian artist turned art critic

Complexity kills. Complexity sucks the life out of users, developers and IT. Complexity makes products difficult to plan, build, test and use. Complexity introduces security challenges. Complexity causes administrator frustration.

—Ray Ozzie, former Microsoft chief architect turned Microsoft critic

Years before he conceived the iPod, iPhone and iPad, Steve Jobs was design-ing videogames for Atari. Jobs hated complicated manuals, saying products needed to be so simple that a stoned freshman could figure them out. The only instructions for the Star Trek game he built for Atari were: "1. Insert quarter. 2. Avoid Klingons." His main demand of iPod, iPhone and iPad product designers was: "Simplify!" If he couldn't figure out how to navigate to something or if it took more than three clicks, he would flip out.

Simplicity isn't only important for the design of gadgets and games; it also directly translates to the adoption and effective use of services. In medicine, compliance with a prescribed treatment regimen is directly cor-related to the simplicity of that regimen. Studies have demonstrated that compliance with a single prescription medication is inversely correlated

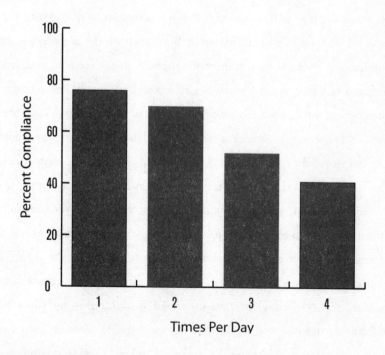

with the number per day: Compliance is cut in half when intake goes from one to four times daily.[14]

The World Health Organization estimates that only about 50 percent of patients in developed countries with chronic diseases are reliably following treatment recommendations.[15] The primary reason for nonadherence is complexity.

If there's one product or service that should be designed so that a stoned freshman can figure it out, it's higher education. Sadly, the traditional seat-time-based higher education model may be the least simple, most complex product or service purportedly designed for mass consumption.

According to research presented at the annual meeting of the American Educational Research Association, if you're trying to earn a degree at a community college, you might as well be going to school at the DMV. Focus groups conducted at Macomb Community College, a two-campus system in Michigan offering over 100 degree programs to 48,000 students, revealed that very few students are able to navigate the complexities of enrollment, financial aid, transcript requests, prior credit recognition, program selection, course selection and scheduling. Faced with so many choices, students either avoid making decisions or make decisions they later regret.[16] For example, "students might select whichever courses are most convenient for their schedule, and then later find out they've wasted their time and money on a course that doesn't count toward their degree . . . For some of them, this could be the last straw that breaks their tenuous attachment to college." This is particularly so when students are enrolled at multiple institutions simultaneously in an attempt to get the requisite courses—something increasingly common as a result of our approach to funding (i.e., rationing) at state-supported institutions—and when 52 percent of students entering community colleges are relegated to remedial courses. James Skidmore, chancellor of the West Virginia community college system, refers to remedial courses as "the quicksand of higher education. Students get in . . . and they never get out."[17]

While the iPod, iPhone and iPad had a single architect (or maybe two) who valued simplicity above all and would stop at nothing to achieve it, product design at colleges and universities is by committee, if there is a coherent design at all. And simplicity isn't a priority for the committee. Moreover, with nearly half of US students enrolled in undergraduate higher education programs at community colleges and 70 percent of total enrollment concentrated at state-supported institutions, it's important to acknowledge that government and government-supported institutions are not renowned for simple products and services.

Complex rules are not only hard to follow; complexity provides our cunning brains with a wide expanse of excuses for not following the rules. It's no wonder nearly half of all students who start college in this country never finish.

It will take a ton of work over the next 20 years to move our higher education system from a seat-time to a competency-based model. But when we do, higher education will be much simpler to navigate and use. Transfer credits and courses that don't apply to your degree will be anachronistic. Competency-based programs will radically lower costs and limit the role and need for financial aid (itself a major source of complexity). Student competencies will be laid bare before prospective employers and matched to job descriptions. Adoption of online learning will soar; dropouts will plummet.

Steve Jobs liked to say simple was a lot harder than complex: "You have to work hard to get your thinking clean to make it simple. But it's worth it in the end because once you get there, you can move mountains."[18] These new institutions will take time and a lot of hard work to build. But competency-based learning will fundamentally transform the seemingly immovable mountain of higher education by allowing online education to move past accessibility to attack affordability and efficacy.

Put differently, the real Wonderland Thrun sighted back in 2012 is where failure is no longer an option. That's the land of competency-based learning. And we don't need a pill to find it.

IMMERSION, FOCUS AND FLOW

When you're learning online, no one can hear you scream . . .

The fundamental drawback of online delivery is trading physical presence in a learning environment for convenience. So what's lost when we're not physically present? If you attended an elite university and resided on campus for a year or more, you probably agree that a great deal if not most of your learning—or at least the learning that stuck—occurred beyond the confines of the classroom. Learning extended into dorm rooms, common rooms and dining halls. Learning came from serendipitous encounters on the quad and study groups. Many who have benefited from these immersive environments fervently believe that the potential for learning outside the college classroom dwarfs what can possibly occur in the classroom.

In ascertaining exactly what is lost, it is helpful to think about successful educational programs that could not possibly work online. For example, Middlebury's famous summer language schools, where arriving students take a language pledge and thereafter are not permitted to communicate in English throughout their enrollment (or risk expulsion). This means that in the classroom, at meals, during extracurricular activities and in the dorm, students have no choice but to focus on the task of mastering the new language. Research has validated this immersion model as the most effective environment for language learning.

The best known immersion model of recent years is one dedicated to solving a problem that's much more important than lack of language skills: endemic poverty. The Harlem Children's Zone (HCZ) has constructed an immersion system of education, social services and community programs within 100 blocks of Central Harlem. The goal is not only to prevent children from dropping out of school, but to help them get to and graduate from college with the tools to succeed in life, thereby breaking the cycle of generational poverty. The program begins with prenatal care and continues to support virtually every aspect of a child's education and health all the way through college. It is intended as a safety net so broad that no matter how and where you fall, you won't fall through. The results to date are extremely promising: Test scores of HCZ middle school students are indistinguishable from scores of more affluent kids. President Obama's Promise Neighborhoods program intends to create 20 children's zones around the country modeled on HCZ.

The consensus on immersion programs like HCZ and Middlebury is that they work but are expensive and therefore cannot be scaled to accommodate the educational needs of more than a small minority of those who could benefit. The same is true of our elite residential universities. This is why it is crucial for online education to become as immersive as possible. If online learning can adopt similar immersion properties, it will become the dominant mode of delivery for higher education.

Unlike immersion programs, online programs cannot control behavior. At any time during an online learning experience, the student has the choice to open a new browser or walk away from the computer. The difference can be summarized as "controlled focus" vs. "focus by choice." In an immersive environment, a student's focus is controlled so virtually no one falls through the cracks.

So the key question online education must answer is how best to design and execute online learning programs to maximize student "focus by choice" to the point that it approximates the "controlled focus" of immersion programs.

Despite the appeal of social learning, the best answer is not to attempt to replicate the campus environment. Rather, instructional designers should pay heed to the example of Michelangelo, who painted the ceiling of the Vatican's Sistine Chapel for days at a time without stopping for food or sleep. Such stories caught the attention of the positive psychologist Mihaly Csikszentmihalyi, former head of the Department of Psychology at the University of Chicago. Csikszentmihalyi developed the theory of flow, which describes the mental state in which a person, working alone, is fully focused and immersed in work. Csikszentmihalyi's work demonstrated that the three key criteria for entering flow are:

1. Highly challenging work;
2. Individual has the sense that his or her skills are above average and more than adequate to succeed with the work; and
3. Goals are clear, and feedback is consistent.

Flow is achieved by artists, musicians, baseball players, and, of course, students. If and when students enter flow, research has demonstrated that their brain is so fully engaged that focus is no longer a matter of choice, it is effectively controlled.

The good news is that, besides competency-based learning, the other two technology-enabled developments that will revolutionize higher education relate directly to flow: adaptive learning and gamification.

ADAPTIVE LEARNING

Why is it that education remains stuck in a seat-time environment? The underlying rationale is that in an instructor-led classroom, the instructor can really only deliver a single stream of instruction. So everyone needs to keep up.

Adaptive learning is technology making the single stream obsolete. When instruction is delivered online, there's no reason every student shouldn't have their own stream, which might progress faster or slower, and likely in a different order. Adaptive learning typically accompanies competency-based learning. But it is distinct. Adaptive learning can be integrated into seat-time models; most students have experienced adaptive software that they might use in a given unit, or for remedial work.

Combining adaptive learning with competency-based learning is the killer app of online education. Students will progress at their own paces. When they excel on formative assessments integrated into the curricula, they are served up more challenging learning objects. And when students struggle, adaptive systems throttle back until they're ready for more. Adaptivity helps students build and maintain confidence, which leads to flow.

Current leaders in adaptive learning are private companies with available capital for these costly systems. In terms of institutions, Apollo, American Public and Career Education have adaptive projects—Apollo after spending nearly $100 million to acquire Carnegie Learning, an adaptive math company, in 2011. Among service providers to traditional institutions, Knewton stands head and shoulders above the rest, largely by dint of the $104 million it has raised from investors.

The advent of tablets and immersive (non-browser-based) app environments will make adaptive learning even more powerful. Tablets know if a student is moving the tablet, touching the screen, whether there is ambient noise, if there is a human facing the screen, location, or change in focus (switching from one program to another). These are called "telemetry data" and are additional inputs as an adaptive learning system determines which learning object to serve up next to the learner.

GAMIFICATION

While competency-based learning and adaptive learning will be the core of future online delivery, the third technology-driven element, gamification, may prove to be the most transformative—making education as addictive as slots. In slots and videogames, goals are clear and feedback is immediate. Focus is the result of interactivity and competition. If you've ever tried to pry a teenager from a game console (or a friend from a slot machine), you've witnessed the power of gamification. Successful next-generation online learning models will employ the gamelike elements of rewards and recognition to provide students with the sense that they can succeed and to propel them onto the next unit, without regard to their ability to stay focused on the long-term goal of earning the degree. We're already seeing promising signals: Kaplan University has integrated gaming elements such as leader boards, challenges and badges into curricula at its School of Information Technology and has seen its failure rates decline by 16 percent and student engagement increase by 10 percent.[19]

Today online learning can't compensate for the self-selection bias. But in a few years it will be a different story. With advances in gamification and adaptive learning, it will be hard to argue that online programs do not produce educational outcomes comparable to all but a handful of elite universities.

We are in the midst of an ed-tech boom the likes of which has not been seen since the late 1990s. But it's critical to understand what technology can do in education and what it can't.

In K-to-12 education, the path of technology has been rocky—from computers in the classroom, to high-speed Internet connections in the classroom, to a laptop for each student, to Smartboards and now iPads—all without any demonstration of measurable outcomes or return on the massive investment. Technology is a tool, not a solution. What matters is how it's used. As a study by Mid-Continent Research for Education and Learning stated: "Good teachers can make good use of computers, while bad teachers won't, and they and their students could wind up becoming distracted by technology."[20]

The same is true in higher education. There are numerous examples of technologies adopted by colleges and universities that have proven to be a distraction because they are not serving student learning.

A good example of where technology is serving learning can be found at the first new medical school to open in New York City in the past 30 years. In its Doctor of Osteopathic Medicine program, the Touro College of Osteopathic Medicine is using technology to rethink how medical education is delivered. Faculty lectures are recorded so students can attend online using Touro's iTunes University account before attending class. Classes focus on Q&A discussions and in-class assessments to ensure that core concepts have been retained. Assessments completed online are returned to students showing which lecture and learning object (with the time code reference) covers the topic in question. Finally, with the much more frequent assessments enabled through lecture capture, Touro is able to map student progress relative to the expected path of former students who have passed the medical boards. Touro now knows at what point divergence from the expected path is predictive of failure to pass the boards and is able to intervene with students at the appropriate point. Not surprisingly, the program is experiencing remarkable success and recently graduated its first class of 100, including 35 under-represented minorities (in stark contrast to the medical school average of 5 percent minority).

Simply put, Touro has used technology to change its model for delivering higher education. And changing the delivery model is almost always necessary in order to generate a return on an investment in technology. For example, providing Internet access in the classroom has proven to be a distraction to learning (just ask any professor). In such cases, the delivery model remains unchanged. On the other hand, Touro's dynamic classroom is an entirely new delivery model that is generating strong returns to student learning on a modest investment.

You've probably heard of large state university systems that have adopted a new Enterprise Resource Planning (ERP) system—e.g., PeopleSoft—and run into difficulties with massive cost overruns from thousands of customizations and resulting service breakdowns. Current conventional wisdom is you're crazy to try to customize an ERP to meet your business processes. The only path is to change your business processes to conform to what the ERP can do. Otherwise, don't bother.

It's the same with teaching and learning. Colleges and universities that don't change their processes to accommodate technology are—like most K-to-12 schools—effectively spending money on computers that will sit in the back of the classroom, ancillary and not contributing to student learning.

On the other hand, colleges and universities that do change their processes—to incorporate gamification and competency-based, adaptive learning that is lower-cost but more effective—are unlikely to look like traditional universities. They will be accredited, they will grant degrees and they will have faculty (of a sort). But they will be better in significant ways that don't simply relate to convenience (anytime, anywhere) and afford-ability. First, they will produce outcomes consistently better than their ana-log antecedents. And to do this, degree programs will have been rethought and delivered differently. Second, like Apple's successful products, they are likely to be more open in encouraging contributions from students, and perhaps nonstudents, in the form of content and apps. The winning de-gree-providers will be those that engender an ecosystem of learning within their virtual campus walls.

At the same time, a university education is not a mobile device. De-grees are credentials that stay with graduates for life. And so the impetus to "Think Different" must be tempered by the realization that the institution cannot be so different that it is no longer recognizable as a university.

Somewhere between stage 1 (accessibility) and stage 3 (efficacy), on-line learning will pass through the stage of full acceptance from all con-stituencies (institutions, students and employers). While the percentage of each concerned about quality in online delivery is declining annually, a healthy minority remains skeptical. Probably the most intractable prejudice remaining on the part of employers doesn't involve form or quality, but rather what I call "the weirdo factor"—i.e., do online students have any social skills or what? Overcoming the weirdo factor will require institutions that still look and sound like universities and that grant credentials that still look and sound like degrees. That is, until The Great Unbundling.

SIX

THE GREAT UNBUNDLING

"With everything that's going on, this is probably the last deb season as we know it."

— "Nick Smith," *Metropolitan*

WHIT STILLMAN'S 1990 FILM *METROPOLITAN* CHRON-icles the adventures—more accurately, elaborate and annoying conversations—of a group of rich, young toffs during debutante ball season. I remember seeing the film with friends during my freshman year. Coming from Canada, the world of *Metropolitan* was foreign and exotic to me. But it was familiar to a few people in our group, one of whom had been a "deb."

Since then, I've been amused by debutantes—17- or 18-year-old women from upper-class families who are "presented" to society at a formal "debut" event, typically called a debutante ball. Historically, these events had a practical purpose: to display young women to eligible bachelors from equally impressive upper-class families, to foster intermarriage and to perpetuate class dominance.

But as Whit Stillman's character notes in the film, debutantes have gone through a rough patch in recent years. Even Prince Philip, a man not known for his progressive views, barred the main London event from being held at Buckingham Palace, calling it "bloody daft."

So the question I've been mulling is this: Will degrees become as impractical and amusing as debutantes? As noted, our colleges and universities are already too much like debutante balls in their failure to promote social mobility; you shouldn't have to be a deb, or know one, to have the opportunities that a great college can provide. But here are two more reasons why this is worth pondering.

1. Return on Investment

Debutante balls are expensive. In order to attend the International Debutante Ball in New York, you have to join the organization and pay a membership fee of $16,000. Dance lessons (waltzing is *de rigueur*) and thousand-dollar dresses add to the cost. The return on this investment in the present day is unclear. Most debutantes seem to view the experience as something they're doing because their mom did it or as a networking opportunity.

Degrees are even more expensive than debutante balls, but many offer a similar return profile. And even though online delivery cuts the cost of delivery in half, few higher education institutions delivering programs online have opted to charge less. Which is kind of daft, not unlike the debutante process.

2. Opacity

Debutantes are "presented" to society, but what does society learn from the process? That girls look good in white dresses? Likewise, degrees don't say very much about the recipient. What is a degree?

A degree signals not one thing but rather an opaque bundle of many things: (1) specific knowledge and skills; (2) general education; (3) the combined specific and general knowledge and skills represented by the selected program of study; (4) the stick-to-it-iveness to complete a multiyear endeavor; (5) certification that the individual met the institution's standards for admission; and (6) that the individual also gained intangible benefits like building a network, fun, athletics and drinking, as well as the personal benefit of having become educated. So even when a job-seeker has a degree, his or her specific knowledge and skills remain unclear.

BUNDLING 101

Although not common parlance in the halls of academia, bundling has been central to the higher education business model for centuries. The degree represents the aforementioned attributes. But to produce these outputs, colleges and universities combine content and functions into a single bundle for which they charge "tuition and fees."

The content bundle includes remedial course work, general education courses and advanced courses in the major. Although certificate programs are growing in popularity, 79 percent of credentials granted by US colleges and universities are two- and four-year degrees, which means the content bundle prohibits students from earning a meaningful credential in less than two years.[1]

But the larger part of the bundle was described in chapter 3: all the things universities have taken on that don't relate to student outcomes. These include real estate, dining, sports, research and the many provinces of deanlets. As Anant Agarwal, president of edX, asks: "Universities are responsible for admissions, research, facilities management, housing, health care, credentialing, food service, athletic facilities, career guidance and placement, and much more. Which of these items should be at the core of a university and add value to that experience?"[2] It's the right question, because while these don't add time-to-credential, as the content bundle does, they add to the cost, which has the same effect on return on investment.

Over the past decade, sales of recorded music are down 50 percent and continue to fall each year. The reason isn't online piracy. It's that digital technology has forced a revolution in a business model that, in the past, had relied on bundling the music young consumers wanted (single songs) with music they didn't (the rest of the album—except for "Sgt. Pepper," and pretty much anything by Van Halen). In an industry unbundled by technology, consumers can purchase only the content that they want and the bundled product is no longer viable.

New entrants in the airline business have unbundled their offerings to reduce fares. While airlines used to include everything in the fare (checked luggage, meals, pillows), discount airlines keep the fares as low as possible, allowing travelers to add products or services if they wish to pay more—and driving many travelers crazy. Some discount airlines charge $50 or more for a boarding pass if customers don't print them at home ahead of time. Ryanair CEO Michael O'Leary once suggested the airline would begin charging customers to use the toilets but backed away after public uproar.

We've seen unbundling in telecommunications (choose the number of minutes on your calling plan) and are now starting to see it with television. Thanks to DVRs and Netflix, we no longer watch channels or networks, but rather individual shows. Many viewers are no longer aware of which networks air their favorite programs. If viewers were given a mechanism for paying only for the shows they watched rather than the thousands they don't, cable bills would collapse, as would the fortunes of Comcast and their brethren.

In microeconomic terms, bundling captures surplus for producers. Unbundling moves much of that producer surplus to consumers and may create new consumer surplus. For higher education, unbundling would drastically reduce revenue per student. As a result, the cost structure of colleges and universities would need to downshift dramatically.

If colleges and universities are forced to unbundle, many will have a dystopian future. For television networks, popular programs support new, innovative and struggling shows. For universities, we might see popular courses and programs thrive while the rest are left to wither on the vine. Institutions might be less willing to take risks on new programs (like computer science and biotechnology once were). In addition, in a world where the higher education consumer is king, it may be challenging to insist on general education requirements, distributional requirements, and the precepts of a liberal arts education.

Bundling has been the primary way universities have managed to forestall these changes and avoid the return on investment analyses consumers make for virtually every other purchase decision. So it's a fair question: Will higher education's next decade be known as The Great Unbundling?

Bundling in any industry is only sustainable if three conditions are met.[3]

Economies of scale in production
Ongoing bundling can be supported when there are efficiencies from producing related but different products together rather than separately. There are two elements to efficiencies: the value of what is being produced and the cost of doing so.

Almost every industry demonstrates cost efficiencies in production of related products. If a music label is already producing bad songs, the marginal cost of producing a hit song will be less than starting from scratch. With universities it's a closer call. The overhead and inefficiencies that most universities have built up in the name of achieving their broad, multi-bottom-line missions may well create diseconomies of scale.

But let's assume that there are still economies on the cost side to delivering French literature degrees alongside chemical engineering degrees. Then the question is whether producing the related products together adds value to the products. In music, a hit song isn't any better because the band that came into the studio the day before laid down a dud. Fundamental to the concept of a university is the notion that new knowledge is created when disciplines rub shoulders, or through serendipitous conversations on the quad—although the extent to which this translates into better learning outcomes for students surely varies by institution. But with the rise of interdisciplinary studies, I believe overall knowledge does experience economies of scale in production. Whether that increased knowledge is effectively transmitted to students as a result of bundling is a harder question.

Heterogeneous demands of consumers
Bundling is more easily sustained when consumers value different parts of the bundle differently. For example, television viewer A might value ESPN at $20 per month and the Food Network at $5 per month, while viewer B might have exactly the reverse preferences. In an unbundled world, if the cable network charges more than $5 for either channel, one of the viewers will refuse to buy it, which may mean that network is no longer available (or, in theory, no longer available with the same level of quality). Only by bundling can sellers and buyers achieve an optimal result. In contrast,

in music, hit songs are hit songs for a reason: Most consumers prefer them and would pay more for them. On the whole, consumers of higher education are more like TV viewers than music buyers; students are undoubtedly heterogeneous in how they value different aspects of the higher education bundle.

Simplification

Bundling tends to persist when consumers appreciate simplifying the purchase decision. This is why we don't buy books by the chapter or newspapers by the article. In higher education, while do-it-yourself (DIY) education was a hot topic a few years ago, demand hasn't come close to meeting the hype. Although students can radically reduce the cost of earning a degree through DIY options like Straighterline, a company that charges as little as $49 per course, the additional work required to get an accredited, degree-granting institution to recognize those credits, fit those credits into the institution's requirements, and complete remaining coursework is too much brain damage for all but motivated nerds who probably have the resources to pay full freight from the outset. There's no evidence to suggest that any meaningful number of students want to be *completely* in charge of their own education.

Based on the classic microeconomic criteria for bundling, it appears as if the practice will reign supreme for the foreseeable future. But just when Joe and Jane College thought they were in the clear, here comes further technological disruption to change the equation.

COMPETENCY MANAGEMENT PLATFORMS

The most fundamental disruption that colleges and universities face in the coming years is not MOOCs or online learning or the useful technologies online learning enables. Rather, it relates to data. Not the work of defining and capturing educational outcome data described in the prior chapter, or even defining signal metrics at the institutional level—those will take years. But rather data that defines the gap between what the labor market is asking for and what higher education is providing. This data is not only available today; it can be analyzed and made useful by commercially available algorithms developed for search engines and other online ventures.

The rise of competency management platforms over the next several years will change the unbundling equation to the disadvantage of colleges and universities. Here's what competency management platforms will allow job seekers to do:

- Upload their resumes and transcripts and—using algorithms honed by terabytes of training data—show them a profile of their competencies across hundreds of criteria.
- Supplement their profiles with short-form assessments on key cognitive skills and behavioral characteristics. After, say, four 15-minute tests, a student's profile might be accurate with 90 percent confidence.
- Point to a goal job or career, which will also have a competency profile attached to it (as a result of algorithmic analyses of thousands of similar job descriptions), and measure the competency gap between where they are and where they want to go.
- Recommend educational options for filling that gap based on available time-to-job. (An 18-year-old will get a different recommendation from a 45-year-old who needs to support her family.)

Then students will be able to map the most efficient path from here to there. And unfortunately for universities, that path is not likely to be a degree. Employers will applaud, as they'll have much greater visibility on a prospective employee's ability to perform in a given job.

Competency management platforms are evolving now for two reasons. First, the source data to connect job seekers, jobs and educational opportunities—i.e., resumes, transcripts, test results, job descriptions, syllabi and course descriptions—are entirely available online, searchable and analyzable. Second, the technology to extract and derive meaning from this data is now available in the form of machine learning and natural language processing.

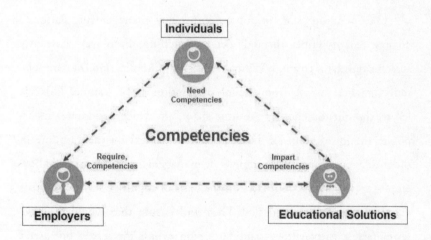

Competency management platforms that function as above will lead to the first human capital marketplaces. While digital marketplaces have revolutionized sectors such as consumer goods, real estate and personal relationships over the past 15 years, there has not yet been a digital marketplace for human capital. Although there are a number of very successful online businesses in these areas (LinkedIn, various jobs sites), none is a true marketplace connecting buyers and sellers in a transparent and actionable way.

The need for a functional human capital marketplace has never been clearer. There are 4.5 million unfilled jobs in the United States at the same time that 12 million Americans are currently looking for a job. Despite job sites that make it much easier to apply for an open position, it now takes twice as long to find a job as it did five years ago. This is mainly due to the fact that recruiters receive twice as many applications for every position and have no additional capability or functionality to sort, classify or prequalify candidates. To date, technology has made hiring more time-consuming for employers.

Like a dating site for jobs, competency management platforms change this dynamic through better matching. Employers currently screen candidates through keyword matching. Application tracking systems match keywords from the job description to the resume. This has led to the phenomenon of "resumé spam," in which candidates incorporate the job description in invisible (white) text on their resumé in order to bypass the filter. Competency management platforms will allow employers to match candidates on the basis of cognitive skills, job skills and behavioral characteristics. They will ensure that employers have fewer false positives (i.e., candidates who bypass the screen but aren't qualified) and false negatives (qualified candidates who are rejected). They will improve the quality of the workforce, reduce turnover and its related costs, and improve productivity. They will become the killer app for hiring.

What does the emergence of competency management platforms do to the criteria for bundling?

Economies of scale in production
No foreseeable impact.

Heterogeneous demands of consumers
If higher education is to be unbundled, consumers need to be able to distinguish the education equivalent of the hit single from all the songs they don't want. Today, flipping through a course catalog, it's difficult for any student to point out the two or three key courses in a particular field.

Competency management platforms will align consumer higher education preferences with labor market needs. Where there are jobs, it will become clear how much they pay and what the requisite competencies are. And while there will still be thousands of different types of jobs, the number of fast-growing jobs will be smaller, and the number of fast-growing, high-paying jobs will be smaller still. The upshot will be to make consumer preferences more homogeneous. There will be greater demand for Ruby-on-Rails coding (open source web framework for programmers) and less for history. More for Spanish and less for French and Italian. Students will be better able to distinguish "hits" from nonhits; higher education will become more of a "hits" business.

Simplification
In the competency management world, students won't have to be *completely* in charge of their own education. They'll be following a path. Granted, that path will be dynamically created by machines rather than handcrafted on an ivy-covered quad. But it will be different and better than the current do-it-yourself path.

Competency management platforms will enable students to assemble learning experiences that will give them the competencies they need for their goal job. They will fill the gap between existing competencies and competencies required by employers effectively and cost-efficiently. While some competency management platforms will undoubtedly make that process complex, the better ones will make it simple. The better ones will also spend millions of dollars to evangelize to employers that when their platform says that a job seeker will exhibit the requisite competencies, employers should take that to the bank. This would make the process of actually getting the job simpler—likely simpler than showing up today at an employer's door with a bundled degree.

EDUCATION-AS-A-SERVICE (EAAS)

"Do you know what Peter Gregory is doing? . . . He's offering $100k to people willing to skip or drop out of college to pursue their idea."

"I don't know what happened to that guy, but he REALLY hates college."

—From HBO series *Silicon Valley*

The HBO series *Silicon Valley* parodies celebrity venture capitalist Peter Thiel with a character named Peter Gregory. Gregory hates college so much that the best strategy for getting him to hear the pitch for your startup is telling him you'll go back to college if he doesn't listen.

Meanwhile, the startups that the real Peter Thiel is backing in the real Silicon Valley are Software-as-a-Service (SaaS) companies. If you're not intimate with SaaS, the exemplar is Salesforce.com. A decade ago, customer relationship management (CRM) required buying, customizing and implementing bulky enterprise software. It was a big-ticket item for most companies, and then every couple of years you'd need to upgrade to the new version. Salesforce.com changed all that. Companies could now "rent" CRM software per user per month. The software (and all the data input by customers) was hosted by Salesforce.com (and now in the cloud). Customers configured the software rather than hiring consultants to customize it to fit their business processes.

Since Salesforce paved the way, hundreds of SaaS startups have bloomed to serve enterprises in every industry at every link of the value chain. But SaaS is also causing incumbent technology providers to change direction. Adobe's primary product used to be the Creative Suite design package, the standard for magazine design and other graphic arts professions. Despite surging global demand for digital graphic design, sales of the $2,600 product were flat. So Adobe launched an SaaS product: Creative Cloud, available for $75 for a single month, or an annual subscription of $50 per month. In the spring of 2013 Adobe announced more than 1.8 million users had signed up for Creative Cloud, growth of more than 400,000 over the prior quarter. Adobe is no longer selling Creative Suite; customers must buy the Creative Cloud.

SaaS companies are growing like topsy and sporting eye-watering multiples. Gartner, a major information technology advisory firm, projects the market for cloud-delivered software and infrastructure will reach $43 billion next year. But this growth isn't being driven by the convenience of paying monthly for access to the same enterprise software businesses used to install on their servers. Instead, SaaS companies are creating real value for customers by unbundling enterprise software into component parts, each of which addresses a discrete customer need. So customers can pay for what they need and no more. One popular new Adobe SaaS product is a $10 per month package aimed at photographers that combines Adobe's design software with an online community to sell photos. No more paying for bloated software, 95 percent of which is never used.

In many respects, colleges and universities are providing the educational equivalent of enterprise software. Current degree offerings are big-ticket items: bulky, requiring several years to complete, and customers pay for the whole thing regardless of what they really need.

Like enterprise software companies, colleges and universities will have to transition from selling degrees to unbundling or providing "Education-as-a-Service" (EaaS). So let's look at what higher education institutions can learn from market leader Salesforce.com.

Table 6.1

Lessons from Salesforce.com[4]	Implications for colleges and universities
Decide on your business model(s) before doing anything else.	Decide whom you're serving, what value you're trying to provide, and who's paying the bill. Certainly not only traditional-age students (and their parents, and the federal government), but also the adult learners who constitute 43 percent of all higher education enrollments. Some employers might want to pay the bill. Keep in mind most leading technology companies already support 5+ discrete business models.
Build the product from day one with a focus on customer experience and value.	Putting a course or degree program online is all well and good, but that's the easy part. EaaS will be about taking advantage of the medium to rethink education. It can't be the same for everyone. Every student has different needs (e.g., motivation, aptitude, preparation, career interest, time-to-job). Follow Adobe's lead and unbundle the degree into component parts to better serve distinct customer profiles and you won't just have a one-time purchase, you'll have a customer for life.

Instill "customer for life" mindset in sales and support, starting with the first sales call; sales needs to be focused on delivering value to the customer vs. generating as much revenue as possible upfront. Salesforce .com's service and support organization is called "Customers for Life" (CFL).

As it was with Adobe, this is scary for colleges and universities. The payoff of EaaS is you really can have Customers for Life. Winning institutions will provide for the ongoing educational needs of their customers. The current distinction between students and alumni slowly will become an anachronism.

Product development must be agile. Salesforce.com issues approximately 500 product releases each year. Such continuous enhancing requires an operations organization (responsible for ensuring the service remains bulletproof) that is separate and distinct from product development.

Faculty will no longer develop a course and teach it the same way for a decade. EaaS will require that learning experiences be kept up-to-date, often with examples pulled from the day's headlines. Also, while colleges and universities are long on "product development" resources (i.e., faculty), they are short on operations. Traditional institutions going online have filled the operations gap through partnerships with service providers. Service providers are likely to play an even more prominent role as operations and delivery become more central to the core value proposition.

Customer service isn't about answering technical queries; the product allows customers to provide self-service. Rather, customer service is about using Salesforce.com to improve the efficiency of the customer's business.

For colleges and universities, customer service will mean helping students optimize the return on their tuition investment. This means better understanding how the institution's offerings prepare students for the specific skills in demand by employers, and then helping students better connect with those employers by making the skills visible to employers or via direct connection to employers.

Rethink governance and leadership structures to make better, faster decisions.

For software companies, the enormity of the challenge in moving to an SaaS model has been huge. For universities—many of which are struggling with the notion of the digital delivery of existing programs—moving to EaaS will be even harder. Perhaps the biggest challenge for most higher education institutions is that current governance structures barely allow them to drive effectively. And when the vehicle heads towards the cliff, the steering mechanism will prove quite inadequate. Winning institutions will be those that streamline governance today for quicker, more effective decision making tomorrow.

Gregory: "Gates, Ellison, Jobs, Dell. All dropped out of college. Silicon Valley is the cradle of innovation because of dropouts. College has become a cruel, expensive joke on the poor and the middle class that benefits only the perpetrators of it: the bloated administrators."

Heckler: "The true value of a college education is intangible."

Gregory: "The true value of snake oil is intangible . . . Do not go back to college. Go work at Burger King. Go into the woods and forage for nuts and berries."

—Peter Gregory giving a TED talk in the *Silicon Valley* series:

Colleges and universities might be well-served to remember the adage: If you can't beat 'em, join 'em. In this case, if you can't convince the Peter Gregorys of the world that you are providing value—and there will be more and more of them in the coming years—become more like the SaaS companies he funds. It's a long road from here to EaaS. But like Adobe, the winning institutions will be those that transition sooner rather than later. Even in Silicon Valley, every journey begins with a single step.

"So many things which were better in the past have been abandoned for supposed convenience."

—"Nick Smith," *Metropolitan*

MOOCs were viewed by some as a sign of unbundling in higher education. Udacity is dogged in its pursuit of Sebastian Thrun's unbundled vision and recently launched "nanodegrees"—compact, hands-on and flexible online IT curricula developed in conjunction with AT&T (but notably without an accredited university behind it). More important signs include one in the UK, where the University of Coventry announced a 50 percent discount, no-frills degree for students willing to accept limited contact hours and no access to IT, the library, athletic facilities or social activities. And, Davidson University in North Carolina, which had washed, dried, folded and ironed students' clothes as part of tuition since 1925 (incoming Davidson students were assigned a laundry number to write on clothes; at reunions, alumni enjoy remembering their laundry numbers) but recently discontinued the service.[5] But competency management platforms—some of which will initially focus on connecting job seekers to jobs, without any immediate link to higher education—are the true sign of the inevitable unbundling to come, and one that many colleges and universities are likely to miss.

Until competency management platforms gain widespread acceptance, "badges" or "stackable credentials" are unlikely to gain much traction. The notion that educated adults, like the boy and girl scouts they once were, will prefer to flaunt a collection of badges testifying to skills they have demonstrated is flawed for one reason. While degrees are validated by a single institution with a recognizable form (i.e., colleges and universities), who is validating a collection of badges? Who vouches that a student has demonstrated a given skill? Although many visionary organizations are seeking to enter this market, outside of IT none currently has the ability or credibility to authenticate such credentials in a way that would be acceptable to a critical mass of employers and students.

In addition, the cost of switching away from degrees is high. Rich Barton founded Expedia and then went on to found Zillow, the real estate site. As Sebastian Thrun observed when I sat with him in his office at Udacity in the summer of 2013, his friend Rich was successful with Expedia in getting consumers to switch from travel agents to booking their own travel because the switching cost was relatively low; if the consumer makes a mistake, it's only a $500 decision. But Rich wasn't as successful with Zillow in convincing consumers to turn away from real estate agents. The reason: If you make a mistake there, it's a much bigger mistake with much higher costs.

Switching away from a degree is an even bigger decision than selling your house—one that stays with you for life. This is the countervailing force that will delay unbundling for a period of time and usher in the next era in higher education: the double-click degree.

DOUBLE-CLICK DEGREES

Double-click degrees are a competency-based system within the current degree framework. As such, they are a way station on the road to unbundling.

While many employers today request college transcripts, particularly for entry-level positions, transcripts are used for degree verification, not to specify competencies or skills that match the employer's needs. This is because transcripts are opaque to employers. No human resources or hiring manager is equipped to decipher a particular transcript from a particular institution. No employer is able to forecast job performance from student transcripts.

Linn State Technical College in Missouri has been doing something different with transcripts for the past five years. After consulting with employers, Linn State determined that the traditional GPA had limited utility. Beyond a B average, employers were much more focused on student outcomes that the college wasn't tracking. So, starting in 2009, alongside GPA, Linn State began reporting a job readiness score for each course. The rubric employed by Linn State faculty includes exactly the skills employers care about: punctuality, interpersonal skills, work habits, trust and citizenship. According to the college, the response from employers was overwhelming.[6]

The Linn State transcript is a forbearer of the coming double-click degree: a degree that is accompanied by a transcript that an employer can double-click on to learn a lot more about the course and the competencies the student has demonstrated.

Technology will be instrumental in this. Students enrolled in double-click degree programs will be on the receiving end of many more formative and summative assessments than are currently delivered. These assessments will allow institutions to correlate competencies to courses, units and learning objects, and thereby unpack the degree. In addition, service providers working with colleges and universities will utilize algorithms to extract competencies from curricula as well as benchmark curricula against other curricula for which competencies have been validated.

But you don't need technology to create a rudimentary double-click degree. Linn State has done so with rubrics and produced a prototype that yields a productive dialogue between employer and prospective employee. By starting with rubrics and then adding technological solutions as they are commercialized, the transcript will become as important to the hiring process as the resumé, and we'll see better matches between employers and prospective employees. The result: more hires, better hires, lower unemployment and higher productivity.

The emergence of the double-click degree holds both promise and peril for colleges and universities. Promise insofar as students, families and policy makers will become increasingly aware of the very tangible value of a degree from an accredited institution of higher learning. Peril in that once the double-click degree becomes common, alternative and emerging credentials have a better chance of competing on a level playing field. Students, families, employers and policy makers may well compare curricula, concepts, skills and competencies, and then opt for the credential with the best return.

As part of the double-click degree, universities will be making underlying work visible so employers won't have to take their word for it; they'll be able to see it for themselves. Electronic portfolios amalgamate and organize student work in a way that is useful for employers and others with an evaluation need. To date, portfolio applications have relied on students or faculty to curate portfolios, which has resulted in poor participation and questionable usefulness (e.g., post one assignment from each class).[7] But allowing employers to see relevant work has great appeal and will emerge as a requirement once learning and course management systems incorporate intelligent, data-driven portfolio applications that tag student work with competency metadata and dynamically create portfolios for each job. Industry leader Blackboard has already announced its Enhanced Cloud Profile, by which students will be able to "display their achievements and skills to potential employers." Blackboard's CEO described the new product as a replacement for the resumé, which "is on its way out."[8]

Of course, electronic portfolios only work if the student work is electronic to begin with, such as on the Blackboard platform. This will prove to be a major advantage of online learning over the next few years. Online students (and hybrid students performing 80 percent or more of their work online) will have portfolios of work that demonstrate exactly the capabilities employers are seeking.

SEVEN

PREPARING FOR THE GREAT UNBUNDLING

Q. How many academics does it take to change a light bulb?

A. Change? Change? Who said anything about CHANGE??[1]

THE GREAT UNBUNDLING IS COMING TO HIGHER education because there is no countervailing force to stop it. This is in stark contrast to K-to-12 education, in which there are over 3.1 million public school teachers.[2] While grade levels, subjects and specialties differ, as homogeneous constituencies go, this one is big. Public school teachers are charged with the instruction of public school students and are notoriously protective of public school funding. They militate against challenges to that funding, their jobs and authority. Most attempts at K-to-12 reform fall into one or more of these categories, and the result is real controversy.

In higher education, there is no such monolithic constituency. In fact, the central figure in higher education is not the full-time tenured faculty member but rather the part-time non-tenure-track adjunct. So while we know who's teaching public school students, most observers are surprised when they learn that over 75 percent of instruction at our colleges and universities is delivered by graduate students, part-time faculty or full-time non-tenure-track faculty.[3]

There are many reasons for this dramatic fact. But its relevance to change in higher education is undeniable: Attempts to galvanize opposition to the changes underway are destined to fall flat. Part-time and adjunct faculty members are primarily interested in more work and steady work. They are likely to be in favor of online programs that have the potential to add enrollment.

Overall, there has been little faculty opposition to the launch of online degree programs at traditional universities. What opposition there is has not received much attention. Even in the University of California system, union concerns and threats about online programs have been met with clear statements from the system that the union has no power whatsoever to block new programs. According to the system, all the union can do is "provide written notice saying, 'We don't like this.'"[4] Elsewhere, opposition has typically been framed in the form of concern around quality, the viability of the business model and—most of all—how much faculty members will be paid.

Not that the media haven't tried to stir the pot. In a 2013 editorial titled "The Trouble with Online College," the *New York Times* dismissed online education as a plaything for the privileged, saying online courses "are inappropriate for struggling students . . . who need close contact with instructors to succeed."[5] Shortly after, *Salon* published "Conservatives Declare War on College" by staff writer Andrew Leonard. In the piece, Leonard concludes that "there is a crucial difference in how the Internet's remaking of higher education is qualitatively different than what we've seen with recorded music and newspapers." That difference, of course, is that *There's a political context to the transformation.* Leonard's logic goes something like this: higher education should be publicly funded; conservatives want to defund higher education; the Republican governors of Texas, Florida and Wisconsin, the "three horsemen of the MOOC apocalypse," are not only seeking to lower the cost of higher education, they are "leading the push to incorporate MOOCs into university curricula." Ergo, MOOCs are a conservative Trojan horse. And, online education is guilty by association, particularly because, according to Leonard, humanities can't be taught online, so an online future means less humanity, more conservatism.[6]

The tone of both pieces is that online education can't be worth a damn. It reminds me of trying to persuade the brilliant Cambridge-educated vice chairman of Warburg Pincus of the potential value of online degrees: Lots of questions about how one could learn without the opportunity to sip sherry with the dons every afternoon. Sadly, sherry-sipping in the common room isn't a relevant benchmark for 95 percent of students enrolled in US higher education.

The *New York Times* editorial may have been driven by the perceived success of its investigation of the virtual schools company K12. The article "Profits and Questions at Online Charter Schools" published in the fall of 2012 caused that company's stock price to fall 25 percent and riled up long-time critics of the company.[7] But the attempt at a repeat in higher education has failed. The Great Unbundling is coming. Will universities be ready?

While employers and students aren't yet clamoring for double-click degrees, let alone uploading their transcripts and resumes to competency management platforms, colleges and universities need to prepare to satisfy students who are increasingly looking for proof of the return on their tuition investment, or how their programs connect to jobs and income.

In this chapter, I outline a series of six strategies colleges and universities should begin pursuing to best meet this demand and position themselves for the Great Unbundling.

1. REFOCUS ACADEMIC PROGRAMS ON COMPETENCIES EMPLOYERS CARE ABOUT

Given the level of resources society devotes to higher education and the reliance of employers on degrees for hiring, one would think that education would be a strong predictor of job readiness—hopefully the strongest. But research shows this is far from the case. The seminal 1984 meta-analysis by John Hunter and Ronda Hunger demonstrated that formal education was actually a relatively poor predictor of job performance, at least as measured by supervisor ratings and work product.[8] M is the mean correlation coefficient for future on-the-job performance. M=0 means no correlation, while M=1 means 100 percent correlation.

The most predictive factor is "ability composite," a combination of three scores on different cognitive skills tests—for example, Applied Mathematics, Reading for Information, and Locating Information. This composite is even more predictive of job performance and success than a job tryout, and over five times more predictive than whether a student has a degree.

It makes perfect sense that students who are better at math and reading are going to be better employees. But becoming better at math and reading—at least as measured by cognitive skills tests—doesn't mean that the solution is higher education as we now know it. Cognitive skills are assessed in a content neutral or independent manner—divorced from the typical learning progression in formal education (e.g., calculus building on algebra). This makes sense as the road to success in most jobs isn't dependent on arriving with any particular knowledge, but rather one's ability to

Table 7.1   Predictors of Job Performance

| | *Validity* | | |
Predictor	M	No. of Studies	Total Subjects
ABILITY COMPOSITE	.53	425	32,124
Job Tryout	.44	20	–
Biographical Inventory	.37	1	4,429
Reference Check	.26	10	5,389
Experience	.18	425	32,124
Interview	.14	10	2,694
Training & Experience Ratings	.13	65	–
Academic Achievement	.11	11	1,089
EDUCATION	.10	425	32,124
Interest	.10	3	1,789
Age	−.01	425	32,124

M = 0 is equivalent to pulling a name out of a hat—no relationship between selection and ultimate performance.
M = 1 is a 100% guarantee that your selection process picked the right guy.
Source: John E. Hunter and Ronda F. Hunter, "Validity and Utility of Alternative Predictors of Job Performance," *Psychological Bulletin* 96, no. 1, 1984. Reproduced by permission of Innovate + Educate.

interpret, sort, organize and make sense of information on the job. This information processing facility is key to success in arriving at a conclusion, developing a product, addressing a customer complaint, or designing a new strategy. Individuals with high levels of cognitive skills are able to move from task to task with high fluidity and productivity. Ironically, given the lack of direct connection to higher education curricula, these cognitive skills are the embodiment of what we think of when we think of a liberal arts education because they represent learning how to learn.

ACT, the leading assessment organization, has profiled over 16,000 jobs by sending experts to corporate work sites and found that over 95 percent of all jobs can be expressed as a combination of three to five fundamental skills, including the three in the ability composite (applied mathematics, reading for information, and locating information). Companies that have utilized cognitive-skills-based hiring to select job candidates have seen fairly remarkable performance improvements, such as 25 to 75 percent reductions in employee churn.

Sounds amazing, right? So amazing it must be illegal? Well, you'd be right about that. It is illegal.

From 1948 to 1981 the federal government employed cognitive skills testing as part of its hiring process. The Federal Service Entrance Examination, one such test, proved very predictive of job performance. But it was also highly discriminatory. Minority groups scored lower on the test. Several lawsuits ensued. On November 19, 1981, in the waning days of the Carter Administration and guided by the Supreme Court's 1971 decision in *Griggs v. Duke Power Co.* which outlawed testing that had a disparate impact on minorities, the federal government signed a consent decree in the case of *Luevano et al. v. Campbell.* The decree prohibited any selection mechanism in hiring that produced "adverse impact" to minority groups. (The 1978 *Uniform Guidelines on Employee Selection Procedures* defined "adverse impact" as a selection rate for any minority group that is less than 80 percent of the rate of the highest scoring group.)[9]

As a result, private sector employers abandoned such testing. Employers who continue to utilize tests that produce adverse impact—not only cognitive skills tests, but also personality tests—are aggressively pursued by the Equal Employment Opportunity Commission (EEOC) until such activity ceases. (Interestingly, neither a federal court nor the EEOC has ever opined on whether using college degrees as a criterion for hiring is in violation of the *Uniform Guidelines.* Given the degree gap faced by minorities, it almost certainly is. But the EEOC employs a literalist reading of the *Griggs* decision and focuses solely on use of assessments, knowing the degree question would open a Pandora's box.)

He guessed as well as he could, and crawled along for a good way, till suddenly his hand met what felt like a tiny ring of cold metal lying on the floor of the tunnel. It was a turning point in his career, but he did not know it.

—J.R.R. Tolkien, *The Hobbit*

As I learned more about the saga of cognitive skills assessments, I imagined how Bilbo Baggins must have felt when he found the ring. Some thought the all-powerful ring could be used for good. But its power was so great it corrupted anyone who slipped it on. In the end, it had to be destroyed, cast into the fires of Mount Doom in Mordor.

But things have changed in the 35 years since the *Uniform Guidelines* have been updated; there should be a path to harnessing the power of cognitive skills assessments for good. Here's what we've learned:

1. Cognitive skills can be remediated reasonably quickly.
Utilizing specific curricula designed to improve cognitive skills in ten hours of training in each of the three key cognitive skills can yield gains of two to three years of full-time education. Moreover, 96 hours of training using the same curricula yielded an improvement so significant that it allowed students to advance an entire job level (e.g., from entry-level to administrative jobs, or from administrative to white-collar jobs). Based on available data, all racial and ethnic groups appear to improve at the same rate.[10]

2. Technology can make cognitive skills tests much more accessible.
The federal government tests were three hours or longer. Through adaptive testing, key cognitive skills can be assessed in a very short

period of time. By shortening the tests, they become repeatable, so candidates can try as many times as they like.

3. Technology can reduce the adverse impact of skills tests.
It has become easier to dynamically generate skills tests for individual jobs that are a combination of cognitive skills and job skills. These tests should produce less adverse impact.

4. Technology can make remediation curricula more effective.
Incorporating adaptive learning, gamification and on-demand help into remediation curricula has the potential to make a very dry and difficult curriculum much more accessible to the students our community colleges are currently failing to serve.

In short, we've learned enough about cognitive skills and the power of technology to help remediate them that we don't need to find a cognitive skills bearer to carry these tests to Mount Doom. By allowing job seekers to repeat tests and by making remediation curriculum more accessible and powerful, adverse impact could be eliminated and assessments made safe and fair for employers and job seekers. (And in the event adverse impact can't be entirely eliminated, you can bet it will be much less than what we currently see from degrees, which will mean better prospects for all students.)

In addition to cognitive skills, employers are fairly clear on what other skills higher education fails to address. For higher level positions, employers feel graduates are lacking written communication skills, verbal communication skills, critical thinking, and complex problem-solving skills; for lower-level positions, the needs should be even easier for colleges to address. According to Peter Cappelli, director of the University of Pennsylvania Wharton School's Center for Human Resources and former co-director of the US Department of Education's National Center on the Educational Quality of the Workforce:

> [The employers'] list is topped not by a cluster of missing technical or academic abilities but by a lack of work attitude and self-management skills such as punctuality, time management, motivation and a strong work ethic. Indeed, the absence of these traits, which used to be called "character issues," repeatedly shows up as a primary concern in numerous studies . . . in 2009, the Business Roundtable conducted a survey asking employers to rank the most important work skills missing among recent high school graduates. Here again, the biggest complaints were about attitudes and self-management skills. We have to go down to the eighth item on the list to find something that might be taught explicitly in schools (oral communication) and fourteenth on the list to find a traditional academic subject (reading skills).[11]

While persevering through four years of college may well build these "character issues" or behavioral skills, a bachelor's degree may not be the most efficient or even effective path to do so. Without focusing assessments on behavioral skills community colleges will never know if their students are job ready, employers won't see improvements, and students won't see an improved return on their tuition investment.

Similarly, higher education also would be well served by assessing students on cognitive skills such as communication, critical thinking and problem solving. Then, using assessment data, institutions could ascertain which programs produce better results, define best practices and propagate them across programs. Focusing on both cognitive and behavioral skills within the context of current degree offerings could prove highly differentiating for universities and highly remunerative for students.

2. AVOID THE PAUSE

I don't spend an undue amount of time in karaoke bars. My failure to adopt this habit is undoubtedly due to the fact that my brother Aaron has a strict policy of performing only gangsta rap songs, which in my humble view are ill-suited to his very, very non-gangsta self.

Nevertheless, when dragged to a sing-along, there is one song I always perform: Prince's legendary "Purple Rain." My shtick is to sing the verse in a ridiculous falsetto ("I never meant to cause you any sorrow"), but at the chorus ("Purple rain, purple rain") immediately descend to the deepest baritone permitted by my vocal cords. The transition from the first verse to chorus invariably gets a laugh, including from my brother who, although he's seen it innumerable times, tries to make me feel good so I won't visibly cringe when he does his inimitable version of Snoop Dogg's "Ain't No Fun (If The Homies Can't Have None)."

There is a tricky part to "Purple Rain." Between the second chorus and the third verse ("Honey I know, I know, I know times are changing"), there is a pause. Early in my career as a Prince impersonator, I tended to milk that pause for as long as the karaoke background track would permit before exploding with screeches of "Honey I know, I know, I know." Then, one evening out in Koreatown with friends from law school at a near-empty karaoke joint—so empty that the young, attractive hostess had joined us and had her arm around one of my friends, while a woman easily old enough to be her mother attempted to drape herself around Aaron—I hit the pause and saw that my audience's attention was elsewhere. The momentum I had came to a screeching halt. Discouraged, I stopped.

There should be a "Pause at Your Own Risk" sign in karaoke bars. And that same sign also should be hung at colleges and universities around the country.

A study out of Florida State University demonstrates that a major source of the persistence gap in higher education is pauses, or terms of nonenrollment. While it may seem tautological to report that failure to complete a degree program is strongly correlated to nonenrollment, consider that a study of 38,000 community college students in Texas revealed that 94 percent pressed pause on their studies at least once. Only about half ever restarted. So this is Exhibit A in explaining why community college completion rates are below 20 percent and why only 53 percent of students who commence programs at four-year institutions ever complete them.[12]

Of equal interest is the fact that a second pause pretty much spells education death. In the Florida State study, fewer than 5 percent of those who paused twice made it through. One pause may be a stop-out; two pauses equals dropout. Despite the lovely shades of purple, the picture is not a pretty one.

The saying "life gets in the way" is a common one in higher education, particularly at community colleges and other institutions that serve adult learners who tend to enroll in part-time or accelerated programs. But this is an excuse we hear too often from our brethren in secondary education—poor outcomes are a result of factors beyond the classroom and therefore beyond our control. Enter innovative educational organizations like KIPP and Harlem Children's Zone: They don't accept that life has to get in the way and are showing remarkable improvements in outcomes and graduation rates.

Likewise, some colleges and universities are deploying strategies to avoid the pause. One is to move students from part-time to full-time. A study from the National Student Clearinghouse Research Center showed

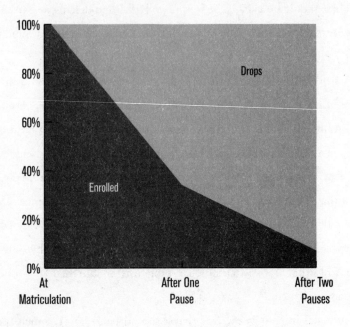

six-year degree completion for part-time students at 20 percent versus 75 percent for full-time students.[13] Clearly, life gets in the way more for part-time students. A study by Public Agenda found that dropouts most frequently cited "juggling work and school" (54 percent) as the cause—much more than affordability (31 percent) or other factors (11 percent or lower). Public Agenda also found that 60 percent of community college students work at least 20 hours per week.[14]

Groups like Complete College America have been focused on this issue, urging higher education institutions to provide incentives to move students from part-time to full-time. This accomplishes two things. First, students complete faster so there's less "life" to "get in the way." Second, full-time students face fewer distractions. City University of New York (CUNY) has pioneered such a program at the associate-degree level and provided a significant incentive for admitted students: free tuition and books. CUNY's full-time Accelerated Study in Associate Programs (ASAP) is producing first-year persistence rates that, in randomized controlled studies, are better by 12 to 25 percent.[15]

While full-time is the optimal solution to avoiding the pause, going to school full-time isn't an option for students who need to continue working to support their families. These students need more structure.

While the best liberal traditions of higher education elevate choice, many students would benefit from less choice. "Students are just radically confused by all the options," said Davis Jenkins of Columbia's Teachers College, as reported in the *Wall Street Journal*.[16] And with students taking more credits than they need due to transferring from one institution to another, more options are resulting in more time for life to get in the way. The *Wall Street Journal* article references the North Carolina Community College system (narrowing first-year options from 77 to 32) and City Colleges of Chicago as examples of less choice and more structure.

A new institution in CUNY, Guttman Community College, requires first-year students to attend full-time, incorporates a summer bridge program and essentially eliminates choice that first year. "If we know that choice shuts many students down," says Guttman's founding president Scott Evenbeck, "why do we so often give them a catalog with 10,000 courses and tell them to pick some?" Guttman retained 75 percent of students in its first year of operation—unprecedented for community colleges with 75 percent of students receiving Pell Grants.[17]

Students will also benefit from more engagement. They will get this as colleges increasingly utilize lecture capture software and systems to transform traditional campus-based courses to hybrid courses. This means not only flipping the classroom (moving lectures online with integrated formative assessments, reserving classroom time for discussion of areas where students have not demonstrated understanding), but instituting dynamic classrooms like at Touro where students are actively engaged during class, providing real-time data to the faculty member on their engagement. Then it will be easy for institutions to aggregate this data into engagement metrics per student, per course and per faculty member.

Additional structure and engagement have the potential to dramatically increase persistence. And that would be something worth singing about.

3. IMPROVE RIGOR

In 2013, Peter Thiel was skewered in a *60 Minutes* profile for his hypocrisy: While encouraging students to drop out or avoid college altogether, he's benefitted from degrees in philosophy and law from Stanford. But several comments made by Thiel Fellowship recipients themselves went "unchallenged" by Morley Safer and his crew:

> Morley Safer: Did you feel that you were being fully challenged when you were at university?
>
> Eden Full: Challenged in the wrong ways. I wasn't challenged in the things that I was interested in and so I struggled a lot.
>
> Sujay Tyle: I was a pre-med student at Harvard. And so I was challenged. But as Eden said, not in the ways I wanted to be.[18]

Thiel's primary critique of higher education is affordability and return on investment. But a secondary critique is that colleges are not challenging students in the ways they want to be challenged. On this point, Thiel could not be more wrong. Being educated does not mean being challenged only in what you're interested in. There is widespread agreement in academe that an educated student, in the words of former Yale President Rick Levin, must have "acquaintance with certain fundamental modes of organizing experience: mathematics, empirical science, historical, philosophical and literary interpretation."[19] Being challenged only in what you're interested in is better characterized as fun than education and is unlikely to constitute a complete education.

While highly structured course requirements were the norm 50 years ago, America's colleges and universities now take a more latitudinarian approach. The demise of rigor in American higher education can be attributed to the fact that colleges and universities are increasingly treating students as customers while, as we have seen, most faculty are happy to focus on research and other pursuits. From the increasing importance placed on student ratings to the need to retain and complete students for college rankings, higher education is increasingly catering to what faculty and students want rather than what students need to be successful in the twenty-first century. Student instruction and learning outcomes must be the core of the higher education mission. But that's an entirely different proposition from treating students as customers. Either students know exactly what's good for them—in which case, they're already educated and, in a poof of logic, colleges and universities have rendered themselves irrelevant—or this line of thinking requires serious peer review.

A short story by Isaac Asimov goes something like this: In a future society education occurs instantaneously through direct computer-brain interface. Brain scans at the age of 18 indicate professional aptitude and—zap—the student is educated and enters the dictated profession. The protagonist dreams of becoming a computer programmer, but when his brain is scanned, he's told his brain is unfit for any form of education and he's sent to a House for the Feeble Minded. After an escape and various adventures, it is revealed that the house is actually an Institute of Higher Studies where original thinking advances science and civilization. The protagonist sets about reconceiving education. People ought to learn in ways other than being zapped and fast-tracked to a profession, such as by reading books and rigorous study and discussion.

The best response higher education can provide to Peter Thiel is to reject zapping and challenge students on exactly what they're not interested in. By embracing rigor, colleges and universities can not only win the digital future globally, but also make progress in addressing the affordability concerns of Thiel and the public at large.

This doesn't mean increasing general education requirements that have no empirical connection to return on investment. It does mean reengineering general education to a program that demonstrably improves the competencies employers care about and then making sure every student who earns a credential from the institution completes that course work.

It also means rethinking so-called practical areas of study like STEM, health, business and education to foster these competencies. One myth that higher education needs to explode is that transformative learning only happens in the humanities. STEM and other disciplines lend themselves just as well to transformative learning.

Developing the creative and critical thinking skills that employers demand is believed to require "perspective transformation" in which students change their frames of reference by critically reflecting on their assumptions. Faculty must assist students in becoming aware and critical of assumptions and provide ample opportunities for oral and written discourse; students must become expert in recognizing frames of reference.

Today many practical majors focus on transmitting knowledge for students to regurgitate on the final exam. Not surprisingly, the students with the worst learning outcomes in the Arum and Roksa study of 2,300 college graduates (discussed in chapter 3) were those in the non-STEM practical majors, like business, communications, and education.[20]

Contrast a typical English class at an average American university with the biology class in the building up the street. In the English class, the subject matter is so accessible that most students can simply reflect on the material from their own frame of reference. In the biology class, students are already asked to reflect on the material through a different frame of reference: a scientific theory that may be foreign to many of them.

So while transformative learning may be more difficult for faculty to achieve in practical subjects, if done well, educational outcomes in practical majors can be even more powerful.

4. MAKE BETTER CONNECTIONS WITH EMPLOYERS

One question I get asked frequently—primarily because I interact with a lot of Germans—is why the United States has been unable to develop the equivalent of the famous German apprenticeship model.

Here's how the German apprenticeship model works. Students attend school one day per week and work at the employer as an apprentice the other four days. The (free or virtually free) vocational academic program lasts two or three years and is intended to prepare students generally for a job in the industry (e.g., automotive), which is typically concentrated in the geographic area. The commitment on the part of employers is to pay minimum wage to students for the time spent on the job. Crucially, employers also engage at the start and end of the process. Students can't commence the vocational academic program until they've secured an apprenticeship at an approved employer. So employers interview and select apprenticeship candidates on the front end. At the back end, they have the option (but not the obligation) to hire apprentices as full-time employees.

Compared to Germany and many other European countries, the United States has always been culturally disadvantaged on this point. In Germany, human resources (HR) is viewed as strategic. HR heads sit on corporate boards and advise CEOs; along with government prodding and support, this has produced high employer engagement in the apprenticeship system. In America, HR doesn't report to the CEO; it's positioned several levels down in the organization. Most companies have attempted to automate hiring in order to reduce HR headcount and costs. Any new investments in human resources need to demonstrate a near-term return on investment.

As for technology, so far it has hurt the cause of employer pre-hire engagement with job seekers. Employers use application tracking systems to create job descriptions and manage applications. Application tracking systems encourage HR and hiring managers to incorporate any and all possible beneficial experience and credentials into job descriptions to the point that many open positions become searches for unicorns; such candidates do not exist. Anecdotes abound of job descriptions that include a surfeit of requirements. For example, a mechanical engineering position that requires three years' experience, working knowledge of various software programs, and the ability to type 65 words per minute. For many positions, requirements have become so detailed and numerous that current employees thriving in the same job wouldn't pass.

At the same time, the ability to apply online means that employers now routinely receive 100 or more applications for every open position, and many are resumé spam. As a result—and as job descriptions get more detailed—employers are getting more false positives in the hiring process. Yet the sheer quantity of applications encourages American employers' fantasy of the "perfect fit." This is an important reason why America has so many unfilled jobs. But it's also why American employers have never been less interested in training new hires. According to a 2011 Accenture survey of US employees, only 21 percent received any employer-provided formal training in the past five years.[21]

On-the-job training is likely the biggest lever America can pull to close the skills gap. Sadly, only a handful of American companies operate anything resembling an apprenticeship program.

Rather than looking to employers, federal and state governments have focused on community colleges that are establishing co-op, internship or workforce training programs in collaboration with local employers. With a community college professor married to the nation's vice president, it's not surprising that community colleges have enjoyed a lengthy and relatively unprecedented moment in the sun during this administration. It's rare that a month goes by without a visit to a community college by the president or vice president. When they visit, they talk about affordability and about community college programs that provide workforce training. The administration has proposed numerous community-college-to-career funds to train people for "high-growth jobs." And in his 2013 State of the Union address, President Barack Obama urged community colleges to work with employers to offer "more apprenticeships that set a young worker on an upward trajectory for life."

The key criteria of apprenticeship programs—harkening back to the German model—are:

- Sufficient industry concentration in the college's geographic area
- A vocational academic program that is generalizable across an industry
- Affordable tuition
- Employers willing to hire part-time interns or apprentices
- Employers willing to engage at the front end of the process

There are a handful of successful community-college-operated programs that meet these five criteria. Several community colleges have a relationship with Pacific Gas and Electric (PG&E) to deliver a PowerPathway program. The program received over 4,000 applications for its first class of 70 (an admission rate of 1.75 percent). The community colleges delivered 12-week courses that have trained over 160 individuals and PG&E estimates its new hires from PowerPathway are six months ahead of other new hires. This translates to a $30,000 savings in time-to-productivity.[22]

The vast majority of community-college-operated programs address the first four criteria, but fail to engage employers until late in the process. For example, Massachusetts' North Shore Community College, is a collaboration between the college and General Electric to train machinists—a "new kind of program that is being closely watched by industry executives and policy makers alike . . . a program connected to the world of work" that guarantees "useful skills" and leads to jobs paying over $60,000.[23] Other workforce training programs in Massachusetts include partnerships between Berkshire Community College and General Dynamics, and between Northern Essex Community College and Raytheon. But none of these engage employers until after students complete the program.

This makes community-college-organized workforce training programs a gamble compared to the German system in which incoming students have employer contact at the start and are reasonably confident they'll obtain a full-time position if they succeed in the program.

The best approach to fill the skills gap is to make a direct connection between an available job and a training opportunity. For example, when the Deepwater Horizon exploded in 2010 resulting in a massive oil spill in the Gulf of Mexico, the Louisiana Community and Technical College system launched a new HAZMAT training program that directly led to thousands of available short-term clean-up jobs; 8,000 students in the

Louisiana system interrupted their programs of study to take this training and get jobs.

Enter the emerging "broker" model. We are seeing the emergence of third parties—typically for-profit companies—that act as brokers between employers and institutions. The broker works with the employer to select an existing certificate or degree program, or to develop a request for proposal (RFP) for a new program based on employer hiring needs and then circulates the RFP to local colleges. Then the broker selects the college, finalizes the curriculum, and returns back to the employer so that the employer can review and then commit to hiring a certain number of graduates from the program.

This job guarantee solves the college's student acquisition model: The institution can market its new program by guaranteeing jobs at defined employers to a certain number of successful completers. The broker is paid by the employer (or the state), typically a fraction of the new hires' wages over a defined period of time. As long as the program produces a strong tuition-to-salary ROI for the student (i.e., the program needs to be affordable), this is a much more scalable model than depending on community colleges to engage employers. All colleges and universities would be well-served to take a hard look at models like this as they emerge. Some private sector schools are already looking to incorporate this employer engagement in order to rekindle enrollment growth.

5. END ISOMORPHISM

As noted earlier, perhaps the most astounding thing about online learning is that it hasn't yet had a material impact on the affordability of degree programs. Content has moved or is moving to be free. But degrees are more expensive than ever for 99 percent of students.

Up to now, higher education has managed to resist the technology-driven cost reductions that have swept through the communications and media sectors (in terms of amount of information or media provided per dollar spent). Fortunately, we see the resistance crumbling.

So here's a top ten list of initiatives I expect to see in the next five years that will reverse the trend toward isomorphism and bend the cost curve for non-elite institutions and make it easier for more of them to offer affordable degree programs. Only half involve technology; the others require business model changes. I've mentioned most of these previously and ordered them here from easy to hard.

1. One-third of all students switch institutions at least once before graduation, and among low-income students, it's over 40 percent. Leading colleges and universities will improve affordability by removing the question of credit transfer and acceptance from faculty and departments. This is a strategic issue that must be dealt with at the institutional level or higher.

2. Flip the classroom; institute dynamic classrooms and increase on-the-ground faculty productivity.

3. Develop online courses priced below on-ground courses for all textbook-based large lecture classes.

4. Shift scholarships back to need-based from merit-based.

5. Increase outsourcing of functions that are not core strengths, including marketing, enrollment, student support, and program delivery to nontraditional students.

6. Disaggregate the role of faculty to achieve development and delivery efficiencies. Specialist faculty will develop courses. Different faculty will provide instruction. Another group will

provide assessment services. Yet another will handle advisement and support. Western Governors University pioneered this model; others are already following.

7. Migrate from a seat-time model to a competency-based model.

8. Move online courses to a self-paced model.

9. Innovate as much with student acquisition as with program delivery. The cost savings opportunity for non-elite institutions in the areas of lead generation and enrollment are nearly as large in program delivery.

10. No more trophy facilities: Spending must be directed to what happens in the classroom rather than on what's easy to admire. Similarly, athletics, extracurricular activities and research must serve learning. If they can't be shown to do so in measurable ways, students should be permitted to opt-out of the deluxe university experience, i.e., these costs should not be included in tuition.

Nearly all of these changes would hurt universities in the rankings. So before embarking on any of these (let alone all of them), colleges and universities will have to take a good, long look in the mirror and decide to make the break. It's not impossible. Look at Harrisburg University of Science and Technology (HUST), an institution established in 2005 after local leaders failed to persuade Pennsylvania's existing universities to open a campus in the state capital. HUST's mission is highly differentiated: to provide a workforce for local tech companies and to try to attract new ones. Of the 115 graduates since its founding, 106 are employed locally. Other differences at HUST: the employer advisory boards vote on curricula, no academic departments, no tenure, and no campus—the university operates from a single building downtown.

6. END "NOT INVENTED HERE" SYNDROME

The 1991 Calhoun College room draw had a major problem. Room configurations for rising sophomores mandated that three different groups of friends combine into a single suite of ten. As a member of one of these groups, I was adamantly opposed to the combine. After all, wasn't one of the privileges of being a sophomore choosing one's roommates?

It all came down to a mediation in the basement of our freshman dorm led by the chair of the Calhoun Rooming Committee and the head freshman counselor. After various mathematical contortions, it became clear that the only way to avoid this fate was if one of our number, an avid sailor, followed through on his intention (sensible at the time, ridiculous in retrospect) to live at the Yale Corinthian Yacht Club. We left the meeting praying to the sailing gods, but it wasn't to be. Ten virtual strangers would be roommates next year in a huge, impersonal two story suite in the top corner of Calhoun.

I spent some time thinking about strategies for making sophomore year tolerable and hit upon BookWorld. A year earlier, Yale's favorite place to buy comic books and soft pornography closed down, and a group of freshmen (now sophomores) had received—in their words—a "five finger discount" on the BookWorld sign. This was no ordinary sign. It was ten-feet long, four-feet high and filled with absurdly long fluorescent bulbs illuminating a sign that gave no indication that the works purveyed weren't of the highest literary caliber. That spring the sign occupied the entire common room of their tiny two-bedroom triple in Branford College. The room, cramped though it was, had obtained some notoriety as BookWorld, and I thought a clear identity and some notoriety could go a long way to help us.

So I approached the group and, upon learning that they had valid title to the sign under an obscure theory of property, paid $90 for it and their help carrying it into Calhoun storage. When September came around and storage revealed its secrets, my new roommates saw what I had in mind. Several were solidly opposed. Most were neutral. Only two shared my vision. Fortunately one, Jon, was a wonderful set designer and builder for various theatrical productions. He immediately saw that by building a very long shelf with angled edges, the sign could be mounted for all of Calhoun to see.

In the spirit of humoring us, everyone kicked in for the shelf construction and Jon got to work. When he was done, Jon engineered the task of raising the shelf and then the sign. Both were dangerous and involved winching it up to the Calhoun castle on the third story, but doing so with safety ropes attached to the bottom to ensure that a sudden gust of wind wouldn't send our new brand identity crashing through the dining hall's stained glass windows. In retrospect, it's amazing we never asked for permission. But no one tried to stop us. A few seniors walked by with eyebrows raised, particularly when the sign was stood on end and passed up two more stories in the stairwell.

The sign raising was so felicitous that we all agreed to follow through on an idea from a passing art history major: celebrate the launch of Book-World with a wine and cheese art opening—each roommate painting his own work inspired by the sign. Again, Jon got to work preparing canvases and the next weekend we attracted more attention as we painted together in the courtyard. The art history major curated the show and wrote descriptions of each painting. The BookWorld opening turned into the social event of the fall. By Christmas, even the naysayers in our group self-identified as BookWorld. The sign had united a disparate group.

A decade later all ten of us were invited back by the Calhoun master to give a talk on the origins of BookWorld. BookWorld had become the most desirable suite in Calhoun and the site of the most memorable parties. The commemorative T-shirt read "BookWorld: 10 years of (Y)ale" with the "Y" crossed out.

Five years after that Calhoun was renovated. The new master was asked what defined the college and needed to be preserved in the renovation. BookWorld was at the top of the list. The architects got to work. They couldn't figure out how we'd gotten the sign up there. An electrician who examined the set-up said it was a death trap. But they went ahead, used a crane to lift a cherry picker into the courtyard and redesigned the suite around the sign. Although the redesign forced the removal of one bed in the suite, it was successful and the sign is now permanently (and safely) affixed to the wall, officially part of Yale's physical plant.

So our search for an identity in 1991 had a lasting effect on Yale—certainly more than if we'd donated money and had a seminar room or weenie bin (a small study carrel in the underground circulating library) named for us; it seems they resell those every few decades. All for the good, I think, except that at a recent reunion, Jon was muttering that, with his luck, the lost bed will mean there won't be room at Yale for his son.

One lesson I take from the story of BookWorld is that most transformative ideas already exist. The hard part is not the idea, but rather the selection and execution. Of the many ironies in American higher education, the most toxic is its combination of isomorphism and the "not-invented-here" syndrome.

The not-invented-here syndrome is the tendency of colleges and universities to develop their own courses, programs, systems and processes rather than looking outside at what works and then doing that. Not-invented-here is understandable: a natural byproduct of intelligent faculty participating in shared governance and exercising academic freedom and intelligent administrators using their best judgment in a loosely managed organization. But it is harmful because it results in services that are delivered less efficiently and effectively. Colleges and universities are trying to achieve the same programmatic outcomes with similar student demographics. If a course, program, system or process works well in one setting, it's highly likely it will work in another.

Colleges and universities are increasingly outsourcing a wide range of functions, primarily to achieve cost savings. According to one recent survey, 60 percent of presidents are looking to outsource more services. But colleges and universities may be overlooking the value of outsourcing functions commonly viewed as core in combating not-invented-here syndrome. Outsourcing typically not only results in cost savings, it can also ensure that the business function in question is delivered in a way that is more likely to be effective—because the service provider likely performs the same function for dozens of other colleges and universities.

If outsourcing proves impossible or implausible for courses, colleges and universities should devote more resources to benchmarking what other institutions are doing and look to conform with their processes and programs when it's clear another school has a better idea. For example, the University of North Texas–Dallas, an institution founded only 13 years ago and therefore less concerned about either isomorphism or the not-invented-here syndrome, engaged Bain Consulting in 2011 to benchmark innovative new models and recommend a new path. The resulting recommendations: online and hybrid delivery of courses, a narrow set of career-oriented majors, larger teaching loads for faculty, and the elimination of the traditional semester in order to "bend the cost curve."

To make our world more of a "BookWorld," colleges and universities would do well to combat not-invented-here syndrome.

EIGHT

AMERICA'S NEXT
GREAT EXPORT

*If you are planning for a year, sow rice. If you are planning for a
decade, plant trees. If you are planning for a lifetime, educate people.*

—Chinese proverb

THE WORST, EXCEPT FOR ALL THE OTHERS

China and other large Asian countries have by far the most vibrant education markets globally. Cultural belief in education as the only vehicle for economic advancement is so strong that Chinese families spend
(depending on the study) between 6 and 20 percent of their income on
education. So with average annual income of $5,000, Chinese families
may be spending as much as $1,000 each year on education.[1] Compare
this to the United States where half of American families report spending NOTHING on education, and you'll understand why many education entrepreneurs believe the most important innovations in education

(including higher education) over the next decade will occur in and for Asian markets.

Many families have come to the United States from China and other Asian countries for the express purpose of educating their children here. So I apologize to them that throughout this book I have recited the following litany of problems facing American higher education:

- Unsustainable cost structure driven by expenditures outside the classroom
- Unaffordable tuition and fees, and uncertain return on investment given the employment market for graduates
- Contributing to the generational wealth gap—now wider than ever
- Locking in social inequality rather than breaking it down
- Arbitrary approach to rationing state subsidies
- Poor job at providing students with basic numeracy and quantitative problem-solving skills
- Poor job at providing graduates with career direction and a sense of how their education relates to future employment
- Lack of consistent and meaningful metrics for student outcomes
- General resistance to innovation

At the same time, the prospects for American higher education are excellent, albeit for a bad reason. As Churchill famously stated: "Democracy is the worst form of government except for all those others that have been tried." The same is true of American higher education.

According to the Academic Ranking of World Universities, 54 of the top 100 universities in the world are in the United States and 11 are in the United Kingdom. Only six are in Asia—five Japanese and one Israeli. No Chinese universities make the list.[2]

One might argue this is to be expected—a natural result of the West's head start in tertiary education. But on the British *Times Higher Education* list of the world's 50 top universities that are less than 50 years old, only 10 are Asian universities, and only one is in Latin America; 13 are in the United States and United Kingdom; none are in Africa. So, if anything, despite what we hear about the United States losing its edge in research, it is preserving its lead in higher education.

Online education has progressed more quickly in America than in any other market, including the United Kingdom. Since all the important innovations in online learning are happening in the United States, should US colleges and universities be preparing to export online degree programs to Asia?

If Asia as a whole had the same tertiary participation rates as America, universities would need to make room for an additional 50 to 100 million students. Meanwhile, the challenges facing Asia's universities—while varied by country—relate to fundamental issues of quality and learning, and therefore are much more difficult to solve:

- **Irrelevant curricula:** Many Asian universities employ outdated and irrelevant curricula, often from as far back as the 1960s, that fail to promote practical skills and critical thinking, let alone engage students.

- **Spoon feeding:** Examinations are often an exercise in regurgitation. India's system is so rote-memorization-oriented that even the most talented students have difficulty passing global examinations that focus on application of concepts (e.g., a CPA exam). A McKinsey Global Institute study found that just 10 percent of Chinese graduates of engineering programs are considered employable in global firms because they lack critical thinking skills.[3]

- **Underfunding:** Salaries of faculty are far too low, classes are overcrowded and there are not enough teaching assistants dedicated to student discussions and support.
- **Cheating:** Because classes are so large and teaching relatively dull, students are disengaged. Cheating is rampant on written assignments and in exams. In India, two students mowed down their teacher in a car (twice!) after he refused to allow their friend to cheat on a matriculation exam. Five Indian judges were caught cheating using smuggled notes while completing a master of law examination. Moving east, in 2006 Ministry of Education and Training inspectors in Vietnam surveyed 2,000 students and found that 89 percent of Vietnamese students admitted to having cheated at some point in their studies.[4] And as faculty are underpaid, it is commonplace for cash to exchange hands from students to faculty—for example, on national holidays when it is appropriate to give gifts.

But the growth in Asian higher education has been driven by China. Chinese higher education enrollment grew at an annual rate of 17 percent between 1998 and 2010. This decade China will produce almost three times the number of college graduates as the United States.

However, this increase in capacity has not yet corresponded to an improvement in global recognition. China (and Asia generally) continue to have scant representation at the top of all global rankings, including the important Shanghai Jiao Tong list. This isn't for lack of trying. A stated goal of Chinese higher education policy has been to elevate its top universities to world-class status. In 2009 the government established the C9, the Chinese Ivy League, including Fudan, Peking, Nanjing, Tsinghua, and Shanghai Jiao Tong. Each university recently received $270 million in government funding and is pulling out all the stops (relocation bonuses as high as $150,000) to draw back "sea turtles"—Chinese PhDs from abroad.[5]

Concerns over quality abound. Complaints at elite universities range from lack of capacity at the C9, which are struggling with surging enrollment ("Good luck trying to find a seat in the library; you can't find a seat even at 3 in the morning"), to more fundamental complaints at the Indian Institute of Technology—shortages of equipment, poor pay for faculty, and quotas that allow students to enroll who can't read or speak English. Plagiarism and the inability to do original work are a dominant concerns. Yale recently terminated a joint undergraduate program with Peking University (PKU) after a Yale faculty member blew the whistle on academic quality. Ecology and evolutionary biology professor Stephen Stearns wrote to his Peking students: "The fact that I have encountered this much plagiarism at PKU tells me something about the behavior of other professors and administrators here. They must tolerate a lot of it, and when they detect it, they cover it up without serious punishment, probably because they do not want to lose face. If they did punish it, it would not be this frequent."[6] A recent Boston Consulting Group survey of the global higher education market assigned points to countries for the strength of their elite universities. The United States again led with 91, followed by the UK with 48. China had 8, India, 6.[7]

The irony is that the returns from elite credentials are probably higher in China than anywhere else. Pressures on Chinese high school students to cram for the *gaokao,* the gateway to the C9 (and nearly all China's universities), are legendary. Private tutoring, already endemic in Japan and Korea, is spreading across China and India. Last year the Chinese media was ablaze with photos of cramming students hooked to energy-boosting IV drips. *The Economist* reported that birth control pills are administered to female students who fear menstruating on test day. But fewer than 0.5

percent of *gaokao* takers will get into the C9.[8] A typical reaction reported in the *Wall Street Journal:* "I placed in the top 10 percent, not good enough to get into the C9. I felt like my life was over."[9] In China, graduates of lower-tier institutions face a hard job hunt; McKinsey Global Institute estimates only 10 percent of Chinese engineering graduates are immediately employable without remediation. The World Economic Forum puts that number at 81 percent for US engineering grads.[10]

Chinese applicants have flooded elite US, UK and Australian universities over the past decade and are now trickling over to non-elites. Because English proficiency is typically the gating factor, many Chinese families who can afford it send their children to boarding schools for the last year or two of high school in order to improve their English and their chances of admission to a top university. Many boarding schools have had to institute unofficial quotas at 10 to 20 percent to ensure Chinese students are integrating into an English-speaking student body and not the other way around.

The past decade has seen an explosion of embedded pathway programs at universities in Australia, the United Kingdom and now the United States. These programs are operated by private providers and guarantee progression into university degree programs if students achieve at the requisite levels in the combination of intensive language instruction and general academic preparedness courses called the foundation year. Market leader INTO University Partnerships Ltd. has signed 18 university partners and reportedly generates over $300 million in revenue from its pathway programs marketed in 30 countries.

Expect to see continued rapid growth of such pathway providers, as well as of the number of Chinese students enrolling directly in US universities. But given the cost of these programs—as much as $50,000 per year plus travel and living expenses—there is a much larger number of Chinese students who would like to earn degrees from US universities, but only if they could pay less and study from home.

DON'T IMPORT STUDENTS:
EXPORT EDUCATION

The answer: online and hybrid learning. The question: How can US universities leverage their lead in online learning to serve students in China and other emerging markets? Multiple questions are wrapped up in this one. The first is whether Chinese students have any interest in learning online at all.

In China and other emerging markets, traditional-age students constitute over 90 percent of the higher education market; capacity constraints in the face of huge demand from traditional-age students render any discussion of the working adult market somewhat pie-in-the-sky at this point.

So we're talking about whether 18-year-old Chinese students have an interest in studying online or through hybrid delivery at US universities. Online programs in China and in other emerging markets are viewed as synonymous with and indistinguishable from traditional correspondence programs. In these markets, correspondence connotes low cost and quality. Most correspondence providers in markets like China and India charge less than $1,000 for an entire credential, which makes quality provision prohibitive, and has heretofore kept US universities out of the market.

Future students in China will decide whether to enroll in on-ground or online programs based on a set of options that fall along perceived value curves. Prior to the emergence of MOOCs, the curves looked like something like this:

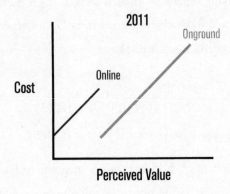

At every tuition level, online programs had significantly less perceived value. At the same cost level as the lowest cost on-ground programs, the perceived value of online programs was probably near zero. And there were no high-cost, high-perceived value online or hybrid programs for undergraduates.

Over the next few years, however, students will see three changes to their online curve:

1. Introduction of lower cost online programs than even the lowest cost on-ground programs
2. Introduction of higher cost online—and particularly hybrid— programs, with higher perceived value
3. Shift of the curve to the right, as online and hybrid programs gain greater perceived value at every tuition level.

This shift to the right will be partly due to a range of new technologies like adaptive learning and gamification that will be incorporated into online programs, enhancing engagement, persistence and student outcomes.

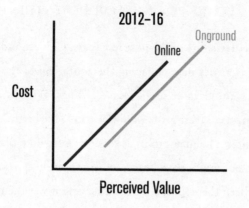

But some of the shift will be due to MOOCs having made online a respectable medium for higher education.

For China and other emerging markets, higher education's singularity happens in the decade after 2017. The online curve will continue to shift to the right. Meanwhile, the on-ground curve will be hinging left below the elite level due to capacity constraints and funding challenges. Also note, online programs of real perceived value will be offered virtually for free.

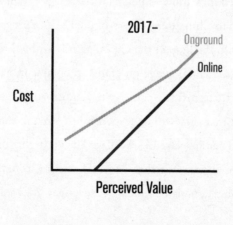

BLACKPOOL BEFORE EASYJET

As the online curve shifts in the next few years, Chinese and other emerging market universities may be facing the equivalent of the UK vacation market back in the days before low-cost airlines. Prior to affordable air travel for the masses, UK tourists would swarm to the best vacation options available in Britain: holiday camps at seaside resorts like Blackpool. In its heyday, Blackpool might have been the best vacation spot in Britain, but anyone who's been there knows that's like saying it was the tallest midget. Once easyJet and Ryanair began offering cheap flights to Majorca and Santorini, Blackpool's days were numbered.

So the question the C9—and all of Chinese higher education—needs to face is this: What happens when Chinese students have access to the easyJets and Ryanairs of higher education, providing affordable transport to the university equivalents of Majorca and Santorini, i.e., the US and UK brands that dominate the global rankings?

Leaders in this market will undoubtedly emerge in this decade. As to what form these market leaders will take, bet on two things. First, that winning programs will be directly relevant to large Asian markets, not simply the same as the programs offered at home. This could mean programs custom-developed for Chinese students with clear program learning objectives meaningful to Chinese employers, or dual-degree programs developed in association with the likes of the C9 (hopefully without the plagiarism). It may also mean dual-language programs: programs in Mandarin, Cantonese or Hindi that provide a pathway to English-language study.

Second, bet that they will be responsive to Vizzini, the self-described Sicilian criminal genius played by Wallace Shawn in the film *The Princess Bride,* who advised hero Westley: "You fell victim to one of the classic blunders, the most famous of which is: Never get involved in a land war in Asia." The easyJets and Ryanairs of higher education will be those that transform the current land war (branch campuses, pathway programs) into an air war—by making affordable online or hybrid programs from world-class US and UK institutions accessible, relevant and appealing to Chinese students.

Capacity constraints and poor quality are not restricted to Asia. These problems are rampant in Latin American and Africa too. One Egyptian faculty member made so much money selling examination questions in exchange for phone cards that he was able to buy a sports car. (He is now in prison.) So while 49 percent of US companies complain about difficulty in filling positions due to lack of skilled candidates, the complaints are as loud or louder in countries like India (53 percent) and Brazil (48 percent).[11]

The bad news is that time flies. The good news is that you're the pilot.

—Chinese proverb

What might exporting education mean for American colleges and universities and the country as a whole? Consider the following: Education is Australia's largest services "export" sector, contributing $13.5 billion to the Australian economy, or roughly 1 percent of GDP.[12] Australia leads the world in higher education exports not because its universities are world-renowned, but because it is closest to Asian markets.

Fast forward to China and India, where online and hybrid degree programs are accepted as equivalent in quality to on-ground programs, where non-elite US universities (along with a smattering of thought-leading elites) offer such degrees for export, and where geographic proximity is nearly meaningless. If the United States was able to generate 1 percent of GDP from the export of online programs, that's $160 billion or about seven times the current US higher education "export market" (i.e., international students studying stateside). It would represent a 30 percent increase in the overall higher education market.

In theory, in a purely online world, the potential could be much larger than Australia's 1 percent. American universities could compete with every Asian university for every Asian student—not simply for those willing to travel abroad. In practice, as average tuition per online student would be much lower than what Chinese students are paying today in Australia, 1 percent is a reasonable target and would make higher education America's largest export, ahead of agriculture and entertainment.

Exporting degrees to emerging markets will become an important revenue stream for many universities. This is not only due to growing unmet demand, but also because the allure of western degrees in emerging markets is likely to persist after (and perhaps long after) the Great Unbundling has altered the landscape of American higher education. Most important, there is no other innovation likely to impact the lives of so many people so fundamentally over the next generation.

GO EAST, YOUNG MAN

A decade from now, which US university will have the largest enrollment of Chinese students in China? So far, elite universities have attempted to have it both ways. They offer MOOCs as outreach, but no meaningful credential. To do so, they fear, would jeopardize their currency (i.e., the degree). For example, MIT named its MOOC platform MITx (now edX). With sufficient resources to do what it likes, Harvard Business School launched a pre–business school curriculum called HBX. Could elite universities succeed in the China market with credentials from X sub-brands?

Colleges today are like airlines 30 years ago when flying the friendly skies cost more than it had to and there was similar grousing aplenty.

When the discount airline model became possible as a result of deregulation, many traditional carriers started their own discount carrier: United begat Shuttle by United and then Ted; Delta begat Delta Express and then Song; USAir begat MetroJet; Air Canada begat Air Canada Tango.

They all failed. They failed because they attempted to leverage the operations of the parent carrier. The traditional operations were hub-and-spoke, while the new discount model worked best point-to-point. The traditional operations had more costly product and process design. Traditional operations were less productive per labor unit (e.g., turnaround time of 45 minutes vs. 20 minutes for new entrants). And traditional operations had labor costs sometimes 50 percent higher than what a new entrant would pay.

Elite universities that attempt to have it both ways by launching credentials into China themselves with a sub-brand will also fail. Highly paid existing faculty will need to be involved. The university may also want to allocate some of its lofty cost structure to the sub-brand. Accreditations will continue to require integration of the new programs with the old infrastructure.

Furthermore, price discrimination will not be an effective tool for selling online or blended programs to Chinese students. If the sticker price seems absurd, students unfamiliar with our unique discounting culture will turn elsewhere. The rising importance of the export opportunity will compel US institutions to join their international brethren and become EDLP (everyday low price) providers rather than discriminators.

Of course, the winning discount airlines weren't sub-brands at all. Southwest in the United States and Ryanair in Europe employed similar strategies: one type of airplane, no meals, no paper tickets, no lounges and online booking only. Both redefined the industry and traditional carriers are still trying to catch up.

So the right question to ask is: Who will be the Southwest Airlines of online education—delivering what customers need, but doing it so much more cost effectively? Odds are against MIT, Harvard, Stanford or an Ivy League university. They are not willing to risk their brands by offering meaningful credentials. So they are playing around the margins, like HBX's pre–business school courses. As Karl Ulrich, vice dean of innovation at University of Pennsylvania Wharton School, observed of HBX, "Those seats are very carefully designed to be off to the side. [HBX is] designed to be not at all threatening to what they're doing at the core of the business school."[13]

The winners will either be private sector universities or traditional universities working with private sector service providers. What they will have in common is a clear vision of educating and granting credentials to millions of qualified students from around the world and a willingness to throw aside existing models. And while you may not have heard of the institutions yet, some of the brands they'll use will ring a bell.

LESSONS IN BRANDING

Brands matter in higher education. Nowhere do they matter more than in China where education entrepreneurs launch universities called "New Cambridge." But existing universities don't have a monopoly on brands that could work in higher education. A new university built in Hebei Province has been described as a replica of Hogwarts from the Harry Potter series.[14] And while I don't see many Chinese students seeking to earn degrees from "Hogwarts University," there are plenty of brands that could attract tens of thousands of Chinese students if combined with degrees from accredited US and UK universities.

How might this work? Think about what happened to carnivals. In 1940 there were an estimated 300 traveling carnivals in the United States. This was the golden age of carnies and roustabouts who ran the games and booths and who'd pitch and tear down concessions and rides as the midways moved from town to town.

Surprise was the carnival's constant theme and attracted millions eager for distraction and amusement. (The term "carnival" is derived from the Latin, literally "to raise the flesh.") Of course, some surprises were more legitimate than others. Fairgoers enjoyed "hanky pank" games (a 5-cent prize for each 50-cent play) and "dark rides" like haunted houses, and often entered through an "Insanitarium" or a funhouse where blasts of air sent skirts overhead and clowns would physically and verbally prod crowds along. Barkers would draw in paying customers to freak show tents featuring "Zip the Pinhead," "Krao, the Missing Link," and Francisco Lentini, the "three-legged boy." Other midway attractions included flea circuses (not fleas, but rather miniature mechanisms for moving tiny wagons and swings) and nudist colonies (girls in the tent wearing skin-colored tights). Or watching a "geek"—the lowest guy on the carny totem pole—who'd perform repulsive acts like biting off the head of a chicken.

Carnies also orchestrated less savory surprises and originated the term "mark"—literally a big spender marked by carnies with powdered chalk on the shoulder. Hence my favorite carny phrase: "always leave the mark a dollar for gas" (so he can get home instead of being stuck at the carnival). Shills were carnies who pretended to be casual players and win big prizes in order to attract marks. One infamous carny surprise was the "key girl" act—selling a mark the key to the room of a female carny, the mark goes to the room only to find a "jealous boyfriend" who shakes down the mark for more money. Stunts like this characterized carnies in popular consciousness as much as their poor hygiene, which the carnies blamed on hard work, long hours and limited bathroom accessibility.

So there are similarities between carnivals and college culture. Surprise! Tuition dollars are subsidizing activities like big-time athletics that aren't producing a return for students. Or surprise! Degrees aren't helping graduates get the job they want, or really any job. Or how about: Surprise! The courses students need to complete their programs aren't available. Surprising outcomes abound in both environments.

Walt Disney was already one of America's most successful entertainment entrepreneurs when he saw the opportunity to send carnies to the showers. The Disney brand was already recognized from his films, and the world's first theme park, Disneyland, featured "book report rides"—literally a retelling of a Disney film—when it opened in 1955. In so doing, he imposed a new order on carny chaos, replacing carnival surprises with theme park delights, particularly for families with young children, a promising market in the postwar era. Most visitors knew the characters, stories, songs and the Disney brand; Cinderella had greater universal appeal than carny surprise. Plus, the overall effect was higher quality entertainment.

Today, carny culture is gone and theme parks dominate the amusement industry, generating nearly $14 billion in revenue each year, of which Disney has 80 percent market share. One of Disney's most ambitious projects of the past few years is the revitalization of Disneyland's underperforming companion park: Disney's California Adventure. Opened in 2001 with attractions inspired by California's culture and geography, the park has now received injections from powerful Disney franchises: Cars Land and new attractions based on *Toy Story* and *The Little Mermaid*. Universal, number two in the theme park market, also builds attractions from known entertainment brands, licensing from films like *Transformers*, *Jurassic Park* and *Spider-Man*. Sticking with the Harry Potter theme, the newest seminal development in the industry is the opening of Universal Orlando's Harry Potter Land. A $265 million re-creation of J.K. Rowling's world complete with Hogwarts Castle, the Dragon Challenge, Hippogriff rides, and authentic butterbeer, Harry Potter Land boosted Universal Orlando attendance by 40 percent. Potter Lands are now being planned for Universal parks in Los Angeles and Japan. A second Orlando park opened in 2014. Not to be outdone, Disney is reorganizing its Orlando Animal Kingdom park around the film *Avatar*. Surprise has been replaced by delight.

Just as the Disney brand and the brands of its film properties resonated strongly in the amusement market, other brands will resonate in the higher education market. For example, Forbes recently licensed its brand to Bridgepoint Education, the for-profit owner of Ashford University, and Ashford rebranded its business school as the Forbes School of Business. That's a brand that would play well in China. In fact, myriad brands that currently have nothing to do with higher education could be useful for institutions interested in developing high-quality programs with higher ROI for students. In the summer of 2013, Condé Nast announced a deal with a company founded by my firm, University Ventures, to associate its brands (*Wired, Vogue, Architectural Digest*) with degree programs. Such brands clearly communicate value to the marketplace and add luster to the brands of universities seeking to export degrees to emerging markets.

But winning institutions will do more than just borrow a world-class brand. Winners will ensure that the resulting branded programs meet and exceed the original brand promise in terms of student outcomes and return on investment. That's exactly what Uncle Walt did. He took a traveling amusement park industry known for workers who were intoxicated or missing teeth and created a paradigm of customer service.

The $160 billion export opportunity for US colleges and universities can make up for a lot of disruption in the domestic market. Capturing any of it will require more than putting programs online and hoping Chinese students will find them. These programs will be tailored for Asian markets. They will be hybrid at first, moving to 100 percent online over time. They will integrate English language training. And they will borrow brands that will add value to the non-elite universities that have the gumption to give it a whirl. Universities that are planning for a lifetime rather than a year or a decade would be well-served to start now.

NINE

MANAGING CHANGE

WHILE UNIVERSITIES NEED TO POINT THEMSELVES
in the right direction to navigate the Great Unbundling, managing the
many changes will require making good decisions every day over the coming years. Higher education leaders will need a distinct set of skills to manage successfully through this disruption. One threshold handicap that
must be overcome is the inertia of "it has always been thus"—a syndrome
that too often fools managers of any enterprise.

BLUE BEADS

The first week of September 1993 was Yale President Rick Levin's first
welcoming address to matriculating freshmen of Yale College. According
to tradition, following the address the president situated himself outside
Woolsey Hall in the Rotunda so that freshmen could shake his hand upon
exiting.

My roommates, my brother Aaron and I decided it was necessary
to provide a special greeting to President Levin and the freshmen. We

sourced 1,500 large blue beads and printed up small cards on thick card stock. The cards had the Yale shield ("Lux et Veritas") up top and read as follows:

> Dear Freshman: For nearly a century, following the Welcoming Address, members of the incoming class have participated in the tradition of meeting the President and passing a small wooden Yale-blue bead into the President's palm when shaking his hand. At the time of your graduation, you will again receive one of the beads exchanged today (perhaps the one you yourself passed to the President), as a reminder of the day you began your Bright College Years.

The beads were Yale-blue. That took hours of calls and visits with nice ladies at Connecticut bead supply stores.

After the speech we positioned ourselves outside the hall and yelled over the din: "Be sure not to leave without your bead. You cannot greet the president without a blue bead." Numbers of panic-stricken freshmen lost their place in the line as they realized they had not received beads.

Back in the hall, a surprised President Levin moved quickly to problem-solving mode—handing the beads to then-dean (now Duke University president) Richard Brodhead for placement in an ever-increasing series of cups, vessels and eventually fish tanks. Levin's daughters played with the beads for a time. They next appeared in the spring of 1997 at a graduation reception for that same class where a sign read, "Come Retrieve Your Blue Bead." The beads were a running joke in the early years of Levin's presidency.

This prank demonstrates not only the power of tradition, it also suggests a path for change. The best way to change something in higher education is to behave as though it has always been thus. This is why the motto of my firm, University Ventures, is "Innovation from within." Waiting on any other kind of innovation in higher education is about as much fun as seeing how high you can count.

As Ann Kirschner, dean of Macaulay Honors College at CUNY, wrote: "The same reverence for tradition that sends graduating seniors walking out through the same gate they entered as freshmen can permeate an institution's entire world view: honoring the past is a hedge against the barbarians of the present."[1]

While the Crisis of Governance makes management tricky, this reverence for tradition makes the task of managing the coming changes doubly difficult for colleges and universities.

FLIGHT FROM FAT SCHOOL

Friday, February 16, 2007, was the day I internalized the vital importance of management. My company, Wellspring, operated boarding schools and summer camps for treating childhood obesity. One of the schools, Wellspring Academy of California, was located in rural central California, just south of Fresno—a town lovingly known as the armpit of the Golden State. The night before, I had received a call from the school's executive director. He informed me that the male English and drama teacher, whom the executive director had terminated earlier that day for providing a secret mobile phone to a female student, had just driven by the campus in his Honda, picked up the female student who had been hiding in the grape fields, and driven away with her.

The teacher himself recounted his passion for this overweight youngster in the tell-it-all, self-published *Fat School Confidential* (buy it on

Amazon, it's a page-turner). He left behind his wife and three-year-old son, promising to take the student to Los Angeles and launch her career in film.

"Bill Moses" (the book's pseudonym for the executive director at Wellspring Academy of California) didn't sleep that night as he and his team attempted to locate the teacher and "Wendy" (pseudonym) and bring her back before the police got involved. Moses had notified Wendy's parents and their patience was waning. The absconding couple made their way from one Denny's to another up and down the Central Valley (the riveting "Flight from Fat School" chapter of the book). In the morning, her mother did call the police. Then Bill received a call from Fox News Fresno, which was in the practice of scanning police radio transmissions: "What can you tell me about your teacher and the kidnapped student?"

The game of cat-and-mouse played itself out six hours later. Bill convinced the teacher to stop at a designated location and sent a van of his top psychologists to attempt to persuade Wendy to come back to the school. The winning argument proved to be: "Is a guy who wouldn't spring for a hotel room last night—the guy who took you from one Denny's to another—really the guy who's going to help you make it in L.A.?" That evening an unkempt Bill Moses faced the Fox News Fresno cameras and spoke eloquently, if wearily, about how glad we all were that Wendy was back where she belonged. The next day Wendy was expelled.

Throughout those 24 hours, it was clear that Bill Moses was in charge. Bill acted decisively, never panicked, communicated clear directions to his team, solved problems creatively, and achieved the desired result of separating Wendy from the teacher. These are the qualities colleges and universities need in their leaders. Not surprisingly, Bill Moses comes off as the villain in *Fat School Confidential* (which would bother me more if I didn't come across so well).

MANAGING THROUGH ADVERSITY

My mentor at Warburg Pincus, the global private equity firm, Rod Moorhead, the legendary founder of Warburg's health care group, had many adages. His favorite—and the one that made the greatest impression on me—is that an investor should only do four things: "Enter an investment, hire the CEO, fire the CEO, and exit the investment." His point wasn't to emphasize the demanding schedule (or lack thereof) of the successful senior private equity professional, but rather that all other decisions are properly the province of the CEO. Investors and directors can make suggestions, but if you're making the decision, you have the wrong CEO. He viewed his many successes through a derivative lens—a result of having chosen the right CEO.

There is a huge need for talented managers to lead our colleges and universities. Unfortunately, there is no commensurate wave of high-potential managers earning PhDs and climbing the ranks of higher education institutions. But I believe that leaders with the qualities of Bill Moses will step up to the task. Adversity has a way of making that happen, in periods of transformative change like revolutions and wars, and even during concerts.

On January 24, 1975, an American jazz pianist named Keith Jarrett was in Germany preparing to play a concert at the Cologne (Köln) Opera House. It was clear to Jarrett this wasn't an ordinary concert. First, he wasn't used to playing opera houses. Second, it was scheduled to begin close to midnight following the conclusion of the earlier opera performance. Third, the concert had been organized by a green, 17-year-old concert promoter. (The promoter's lack of pull accounted for the late start.) Fourth, he was exhausted. He had arrived at the opera house in the late afternoon after a long drive from Zurich. He hadn't slept well in days due to back pain.

Finally, when Jarrett arrived, he saw the piano onstage was not the one he had requested. He had asked for a Bösendorfer 290 Imperial concert grand piano. But his jazz roadies had put a much smaller Bösendorfer baby grand piano onstage and it was too late to do anything about it.

As Jarrett put on his back brace and began warming up, he realized the smaller piano was in lousy shape. Even after tuning, the piano was tinny and thin in the upper registers and weak in the bass. The pedals were barely functional. Jarrett began fighting with the young promoter, saying he wouldn't go on. But the promoter prevailed upon him, saying over 1,400 people were expected to attend; she had sold out the opera house.

Late that night with an eager audience settled in their seats, Jarrett took the stage and immediately demonstrated this would be no ordinary concert. He began by quoting the melody of the opera house signal bell that announced the beginning of the concert. The audience chuckled. Then he went on to one of the most virtuosic improvisational performances ever recorded. He would improvise on one or two chords for extended periods of time. In the first part, he spent almost 12 minutes vamping between A minor 7 and G major. Instead of rolling out chord sequences like most jazz solos, Jarrett rhythmically, repeatedly, almost hypnotically set out one hook after another, creating a novel organic feel.[2]

Later, Jarrett said he had no choice but to play in this way. The poor piano required him to concentrate in the middle register. In addition, Jarrett compensated for the poor quality of the bass on the piano with ostinatos and rolling left-hand rhythmic figures, amplifying the power of the performance.

The Köln Concert became the best-selling solo piano album and best-selling solo jazz album ever. Jarrett attracted legions of fans for whom his music seemed to have a spiritual power. Nearly all attributed their devotion to this one powerful album. In hindsight, Jarrett agrees his performance was achieved only as a result of the adversity he was facing. As the producer of the album, Manfred Eicher, later said, "He played it the way he did because it was not a good piano. Because he could not fall in love with the sound of it, he found another way to get the most out of it."[3]

Fast forward 27 years to the academic world. Michael Crow was contemplating a career move. A dynamic executive vice provost at Columbia University who oversaw Columbia's remarkably successful technology transfer function, Crow was on the short list of every university with an open presidential position.

But rather than choosing the higher education equivalent of the Bösendorfer 290 Imperial concert grand, he moved from New York to Phoenix to assume the presidency of Arizona State University. Higher education cognoscenti questioned his judgment. Long recognized as one of America's top party schools, ASU had scant tradition of excellence in higher education. But President Crow recognized that Arizona could be ground zero for building what he conceived of as the New American University.

ASU under President Crow has been hamstrung by declining state appropriations. During his tenure, state support for ASU has declined 40 percent in real terms.[4] At the same time, he recognized the opportunity to do much more with much less and provide a much-needed model for all public universities.

In the face of this adversity, Crow convinced the many constituencies at ASU to play ball and the result has been the most thorough transformation of any university in memory. He reorganized the university from the traditional departmental model by establishing more than a dozen interdisciplinary schools to focus on solving major social challenges such as renewable energy, urban development and national security. Research spending is up 200 percent and technology transfer revenue has gone from near-zero to $30 million.[5]

While total enrollment has increased by over 50 percent, degrees granted are up 60 percent, demonstrating a real improvement in persistence and completion. ASU now graduates more engineers than MIT and Caltech combined. Remarkably, ASU is now third in Fulbright scholars—ahead of Yale and Columbia.[6] And, ASU now attracts more National Merit scholars than Berkeley or UCLA. Many surveys now list ASU among America's top universities, a remarkable exception to the historical stasis of the rankings.[7]

At the same time, compared to a decade ago, the number of minority students is up by nearly two-thirds to 33 percent in total, accurately reflecting the population of Arizona. Enrollment of low-income Arizona freshmen is up 647 percent;[8] 40 percent of ASU students are Pell-eligible, a 182 percent increase in a decade; and 36 percent are first-generation college students.

ASU has also led the way in terms of public-private partnerships. The university partnered with Knewton to deliver freshman math courses on an adaptive learning platform. This has contributed to a freshman retention rate increase of more than 10 percent.[9] Crow also developed a unique structure for the university's new online arm, ASU Online. Outsourcing to Pearson all non-academic functions involved in online delivery (technology platform, enrollment services) has allowed ASU to focus its efforts on making online learning core to the institution. As such, new programs aren't mandated from the center but rather proposed by departments. Departments are responsible for identifying instructors for their online programs and share in the revenue these programs generate. So rather than focusing online efforts in one part of the university, online is infusing the university, helping all of it to grow.

While most of us wouldn't intentionally choose to play a tinny piano, a tinny piano can be the mother of innovation. One reason I like Mike Crow is that isomorphism is a pet peeve of his. Here's Crow on isomorphism:

If everyone is isomorphic in their thinking, they think their job is to replicate other institutions and to pursue those that are offering the same services but just trying to offer them a little better or in a better environment. To me that is a crushing force against innovation and adaptation because then everything is driven by the leader. Then there really are no innovations and no adaptations to changes because the leader sits in a different environment than all the other institutions sit in.[10]

Few college and university presidents have had to deal with the severe challenges Mike Crow has encountered. (Fewer still have had a Keith Jarrett-like experience.) In the coming years, adversity in multiple forms will confront campuses around the country: demand for affordability, the effects of technological disruption and globalization, and the need to quickly shrink the gap between labor market needs and what higher education needs to provide. So, many college and university presidents will have a Jarrett- or Crow-like moment.

LEADING WITH HUMILITY

One of the keys to successfully navigating these moments is a different style and approach from that of the traditional imperial university president.

One of my family's favorite restaurants is a neighborhood Italian place that can best be described as cheesy. My boys love it because they get to watch the chef make pizza. I love it because the boys are occupied and because my favorite poster hangs in the men's room. The poster is called the "Pope Chart" and, according to Amazon, "features a medallion-sized image and a short biography of every pope; Peter and his 265 successors," though it is not yet updated to include Pope Francis (it is currently out of stock).

Not surprisingly, over two millennia there have been a number of popes whose achievements, according to the Pope Chart, are less than stellar. Here is the Underwhelming Pope Chart I scribbled on a paper towel recently while waiting for one of my boys to finish:

Table 9.1

Pope #	Name	Achievement
11	St. Anicetus	Decreed that the clergy should not have long hair.
14	St. Victor	Decreed that, in Baptism, any kind of water could be used in an emergency.
46	St. Hillary	Decided that a certain level of culture was required to become a priest.
87	Sisinnius	Little noteworthy to report, given that he served on the throne of St. Peter from January 15 to February 4 in the year 708.
133	John XIII	Introduced custom of giving names to bells.
183	Clement IV	Before being a priest and a bishop he was a "man of the world." (Wink, wink, nudge, nudge, say no more.)
186	Gregory X	Elected after a three-year conclave that only concluded because the people removed the roof and put the cardinals on bread and water.
194	Benedict XI	Died after eating a poisoned fig, "a fruit of which he was particularly fond."
215	Pius III	Gout forced him to celebrate mass while seated.

My interest in the Catholic Church extends beyond the Pope Chart. The church is the only institution in the western world older than universities. It also founded many of the earliest universities. Pope #96, St. Leo III, founded the Palatine School, which became the University of Paris, and Pope #195, Clement V, founded the University of Oxford. Most important, like traditional colleges, the church must continue to evolve to meet the needs of the modern era.

The Pope Chart is instructive as to the two keys to reform. First, many of the most successful popes focused on directly serving the church's customers. They mobilized the resources of the church to provide the greatest value to the greatest number of parishioners—mostly poor and working-class Catholics.

Second, the best popes led with humility. By humility, I don't mean Pope #110, Steven V, who "on hearing of his election, barricaded himself inside his house, but the doors were broken open by force" and he was elected. That's more about fear than humility; this was an era when there were few more dangerous professions than pope.

In my mind, leading with humility is exemplified by the current pope, Pope Francis. Francis has opted out of the Papal Palace to live in a modest guest apartment, has distinguished himself from prior popes by washing the feet of the poor, infirm and homeless, and has asked, on the question of gay priests, "if someone is gay and he searches for the Lord and has good will, who am I to judge?"

In doing so, Pope Francis has signaled to the famously inflexible Vatican bureaucracy that he is so serious about reforming the church to better deliver value to parishioners that he puts himself and his high office below their needs. After only one year in office, Pope Francis has achieved a popularity with youth and those not typically drawn to organized religion in a way that eluded his predecessors.

Francis's success is reflected in the phenomenon of Sister Cristina, a nun in full habit who entered as a contestant on the Italian version of the reality television show "The Voice" in the spring of 2014. Her debut was an earth-shattering version of "No One" by Alicia Keys. From that one performance, she became an international phenomenon. Under the tutelage of her coach, Italian rapper J-Ax, Sister Cristina advanced through the competition, belting out Cyndi Lauper and Mariah Carey songs and singing "Can't Get You Out of My Head" with Kylie Minogue. For his part, J-Ax, a sinister-looking character and the first judge to hit the button for Sister Cristina (and spin around to view the singer—the show's conceit), began to cry as the judges discussed her performance. After Sister Cristina chose J-Ax as her coach, J-Ax promised Sister Cristina's mother superior he would protect her from evil and has talked about a rekindled interest in the church. In the finale, Sister Cristina won the competition by singing "Flashdance (What a Feeling)" backed by a troupe of dancing monks (until the monks shook off their cloaks, revealing fluorescent suits). Thanks to Pope Francis's leadership, faith has become cool again.[11] What a feeling, indeed.

Higher education institutions could learn something from watching what's going on in Rome. Changes are coming quickly, and in an era when Bible study has already moved online,[12] colleges and universities don't have much time to change priorities to focus on maximizing value for tuition-paying students. Likewise, presidents may not have much time to adjust leadership style to drive the necessary changes through their institutions. Unfortunately, those that don't may someday find themselves historical relics on a chart on a bathroom wall.

TEN

A TALE OF TWO CITIES?

MANY OF THE CHALLENGES FACING COLLEGES AND universities are best addressed—and will be addressed—through the involvement of the private sector. But like traditional colleges and universities, companies involved in higher education are in the midst of a major transition.

THE BEST OF TIMES, THE WORST OF TIMES

It is the best of times for small private companies aspiring to help colleges and universities deliver online programs, integrate adaptive learning, launch double-click degrees, match students with jobs, and to do many other things. At the ASU + GSV Education Innovation Summit held each April in Phoenix, you can't throw a rock without hitting a private company CEO dealing with the high-class problem of too many meetings with prospective investors. The 2014 gathering attracted over 2,000 attendees and was sold out weeks in advance. By University Venture's count, there were 50 financings or acquisitions of higher education private sector companies in 2013, up 50 percent from 2011 and well ahead of the dot-com peak of 25 deals in 1999. We've also seen the emergence of EdSurge, an online news resource that covers financings of private education companies in the aptly named KA'CHING section of its weekly newsletter. Articles like "Why VCs [venture capitalists] can't afford to ignore EdTech any longer" are appearing in VentureBeat.

Meanwhile, it is the worst of times for public companies like Apollo (parent of University of Phoenix), DeVry, and 12 other public companies that own and operate universities. Over the past quarter century, public companies have contributed the lion's share of new capital and capacity into American higher education. But for the past five years the Department of Education, the media and now state attorneys general have all highlighted the disparity between the rosy marketing of these for-profit certificate and degree programs and the harsh reality that many students have encountered. Total enrollment at University of Phoenix, Career Education and others has declined as much as 50 percent. New enrollments have continued on a negative year-over-year trend that has proven difficult to reverse.

Some of the decline in demand is due to negative consumer perceptions driven by the headlines. Some is due to the same trend afflicting traditional institutions: prospective students' unwillingness to take on debt, particularly for relatively undifferentiated degree programs. But much of the decline can be attributed to protective self-regulation, i.e., filtering out marginal students to improve student outcomes. Short-sellers have made so much money on the sector that they've taken a breather. As far as investors are concerned, postsecondary public companies remain in critical condition. Prompted by the Department of Education (ED), Corinthian has sold its non-Californian campuses to ECMC. a not-for-profit student loan processor. ITT may not be far behind. Many investment analysts have dropped coverage. The CEOs of Apollo Group and DeVry don't bother to make appearances at the Education Innovation Summit. And you don't read about them in KA'CHING or anywhere in EdSurge. To continue with the Dickensian French revolution analogy, these public companies are like the early revolutionary figures that were guillotined and replaced with less unsavory, more charismatic leaders.

Although London and Paris experienced the best and worst of times during the French Revolution, that didn't last. Before too long, *liberté, égalité, fraternité et violence extrême* washed over Europe. Soon, Paris's problems became London's, and London restored a more natural order in Paris. So it will be in higher education; this tale of two cities won't last, at least not for market leaders like Apollo and DeVry. While Silicon Valley education technology companies have garnered headlines and plaudits, for my money the most innovative higher ed technology is being developed inside the public companies.

Consider the fact that Apollo has an annual technology research and development budget estimated to be in excess of $100 million. Or that Capella now owns Sophia, a low-cost provider of online self-paced general education courses, and was the first institution to receive approval of the Higher Learning Commission (North Central Association of Colleges and Schools) to launch competency-based direct assessment programs.

As the largest online universities, the public companies are far ahead of all other institutions in collecting and analyzing data to gain insights on improving student outcomes. Nearly all traditional colleges and universities focus on what's easy to measure (the four Rs) rather than student learning and employment. Having never focused on the four Rs, the public companies have been working on big-data initiatives. With big data, they can identify key inputs and variables and devise tactical, just-in-time interventions to improve student persistence and outcomes. The large online institutions track every click and page view. As adaptive learning comes to the fore, the most effective adaptive systems will be those with the most data, constantly judging which learning object to deliver to which student in which sequence.

Moreover, several of the public companies already have significant international experience and operations. DeVry's success in Brazil is a model for others to follow. Apollo recently acquired a university in South Africa and is chasing institutions in other markets. International expansion requires resources and networks that small private companies will be hard pressed to match. Laureate—far and away the leader in international higher education with 75 institutions in 30 countries enrolling over 800,000 students—hopes to join the ranks of public companies.

Finally, these public companies have a great deal of cash—$2.3 billion in total, nearly as much as the cumulative $2.6 billion invested in higher education from 1995 through 2011.

Table 10.1

Company	Cash in millions as of June 2014
Apollo Group	$645.9
DeVry	$396.8
Career Education	$264.2
Bridgepoint	$219.4
ITT	$218.2
Education Management	$177.5
Strayer	$126.2
American Public	$99.7
Capella	$93.6
Grand Canyon	$39.1
UTI	$34.3
Corinthian	$28.0
TOTAL	$2,343.0

If you look closely at the annual Education Innovation Summit, you will see a few public company CEOs. But instead of sitting on industry panels, they are outside on the patio meeting with private companies. Why? These CEOs need new growth engines for their businesses, and the innovation occurring at private companies is very attractive. Fueled by available cash, public companies likely value innovative private companies more highly than financial investors do. Many of these investments will be acquisitions, but as American Public's investment in Fidelis (a student guidance and support system) has shown, some companies will happily make minority investments and leverage the expertise and resources of private companies while gaining an option to acquire the business down the road.

Those in the business of for-profit higher education might stop being Dickensian in their thinking. It's not a tale of two cities, but rather a single city. Just as the French survived the revolution, the public companies have survived their own revolutions (in government and the media) and the short sellers. Having done so, these companies are in the midst of figuring out an important role to play in the future of global higher education.

The big challenge for the public companies is that many of the significant near-term opportunities involve collaboration with traditional colleges and universities. That's where 90 percent of the students are in the United States, and close to 100 percent around the globe. But as a result of the negative headlines garnered by some public companies, no traditional college wants to be caught out with someone who's just been guillotined—it's too messy. As a result, public companies find themselves poorly positioned for these opportunities. This is more acute for domestic partnerships or service provider opportunities than international ones. But international opportunities are no slam dunk either. Headlines about the troubles of these companies have appeared on every continent except Antarctica, which still awaits its first higher education institution (a personal ambition of mine).

Public companies should focus on sequencing the many opportunities ahead of them. The first step is increasing investment in high return-on-investment programs that don't involve partnership or service provision to traditional universities. By rebuilding their reputations with successful endeavors that demonstrate they are capable of achieving double bottom-line success—that is, student outcomes in addition to financial returns—they will reoccupy prominent positions in the increasingly revolutionary landscape.

FOR-PROFITS VS. NOT-FOR-PROFITS

Those not involved in for-profit higher education should care about this for two reasons. First, traditional colleges and universities need a great deal of help navigating the Great Unbundling—and it's help the private sector is best positioned to provide. And second, the upstart for-profit institutions of today are the traditional universities of tomorrow.

We began with the premise that what makes our system of higher education exceptional is its diversity. Much of this diversity is a product of our rich tradition of private universities. American private not-for-profit universities date back over 300 years to our first colleges: Harvard, William & Mary, Yale, and then most of the rest of the Ivies in the eighteenth century. Today, there are twice as many private institutions as public. At the same time, private not-for-profit higher education dominates countries like Japan, Taiwan, South Korea, the Philippines and Indonesia, where approximately 80 percent of all students attend private higher education institutions.

In this regard, the driver of American higher education's diversity is the maturity of its private not-for-profit universities. This turns out to be key to understanding the fundamental challenge facing for-profit universities.

One of the most cogent responses to the regulatory and media attacks on for-profit universities came from DeVry CEO Daniel Hamburger who attempted to draw a clear analogy between the behavior of for-profit institutions and private not-for-profit institutions like Harvard and Yale, which aim to generate a profit each year but call it a surplus. Why then should for-profits receive discriminatory treatment not only in the tax code, but in direct (and increasing) regulations that only impact for-profit institutions?

While many in the for-profit sector applauded Mr. Hamburger's logic, few outside the sector paid any heed. Mr. Hamburger's argument would have had much greater success in emerging markets like India and Brazil, where private "not-for-profit" institutions exhibit "for-profit" behavior.

Look at Amity University in India. Probably the fastest growing private university in India, Amity was founded 16 years ago by Ashok Chauhan. The university has over 100,000 students. Critics say the university's revenue, estimated to be in the half-billion dollar range, supports a lavish lifestyle for the Chauhan family. While that's unsubstantiated, we do know that Chauhan's birthday is celebrated at his namesake university with a month-long sports festival, and his wife's birthday is the basis for a week-long conference on human values. Moreover, Chauhan has appointed his son as chancellor and says he expects his family to control the university for generations to come. Many other family-founded private universities in India have been criticized for the same cost and value issues that spawned the for-profit pushback in the United States (e.g., "blurring the lines between philanthropy and business").[1]

In Brazil, 32 percent of students attend private for-profit institutions and 42 percent attend private not-for-profit institutions, virtually all of which have been founded in the past 40 years.[2] The analogy here is even clearer. Despite for-profit growth that at its peak has exceeded that of the US institutions, few in the Brazilian for-profit sector are sweating a US-style crackdown. Some argue that this is due to the size and relative importance of the sector. But the best explanation is the fluidity between private not-for-profits and for-profits in Brazil.

It's widely recognized in Brazil that founders of private universities are living the high life off the backs of their universities through "funds siphoned off to associated foundations, and vast salaries paid to management and directors."[3] Private not-for-profit institutions are supposed to allocate 20 percent of their revenue to scholarships but rarely do so. Many of the large for-profits are converted private not-for-profit universities. This explains why Brazilian regulators focus more on the distinction between public and "private" institutions (including for-profits in the definition) than between private not-for-profits and for-profits. And so, in stark contrast to the United States, there is no meaningful legislative, regulatory or—crucially—consumer distinction between private not-for-profits and for-profits.

In contrast, American views of private universities are fixed by the era of their founding, and the subsequent time elapsed. Our most prominent private universities were founded in the eighteenth and nineteenth centuries, a time when few looked upon higher education as a business or means of support for one's family (let alone as a way to build a dynasty). Higher education was viewed solely as a charitable endeavor: worthy of a bequest, not a business plan. This, in combination with their founding by religious groups, was the basis for the establishment of all our top private universities, including those established in the late nineteenth century like Stanford and Chicago.

Over time, control of the private university passed quickly to an independent governing board even if the founder or founding donor was still alive at the time (like Rockefeller with University of Chicago). Such boards would make and approve decisions based on a defined (albeit not always clear) philanthropic mission. Thus the American public's confidence in private universities was established and solidified. It has solidified to the point that "surplus" (to use Hamburger's terminology) scandals like the recent dust-up at Stevens Institute of Technology (whose president was given an illegal $1.8 million low-interest loan to buy a vacation home)[4] or Louis XIV-esque spending by the former president of American University ($200 thousand in redecorating, French chef, tuxedoed waiters and a $22,000 first class plane ticket to Nigeria)[5] bounce off the now-bulletproof edifice of our private colleges and universities.

In the spirit of my favorite equation—tragedy + time = comedy—the right way to think about this is something like:

Although American for-profit institutions have been around since the nineteenth century, until the 1980s and 1990s they lived quiet, unassuming lives as vocational or trade schools. As such, the for-profit university is nearly as young in the United States as in Brazil. The difference is that Brazilian for-profits are perceived as no different from Brazil's equally young private universities, while American for-profits are viewed as on a different planet from the now august private not-for-profit universities that constitute the firmament of American higher education.

It will be interesting to see whether Grand Canyon University can be successful in crossing this chasm between for-profit and private not-for-profit—an ambition evident in that institution's adoption of the trappings of private universities (campuses for traditional age students, participation in NCAA Division I basketball). But many for-profits will be better served by seeking new growth outside the United States, where they may well look like Harvard or Yale compared with many of the new family-owned, surplus-generating private universities. This is exactly what Hamburger and DeVry have been doing in Brazil.

50 SHADES OF DISTRIBUTION

Returning to the "best of times" enjoyed by private companies, most of the exuberance at the Education Innovation Summit surrounds edtech companies, i.e., companies in the business of providing some kind of technology-based educational product or service either to schools or directly to students.

For those who survived the last boom and lived to tell the tale, enthusiasm for edtech is invariably mixed with caution. First, we must distinguish between companies that sell technology to schools and companies that use technology to sell education directly to students. Technology-selling companies have been a dog's breakfast in K-to-12 and not much better in higher education. In fact, Blackboard, the dominant learning management system, is the only major new tech success in higher education.

Education is a seductive market to would-be education entrepreneurs, hundreds of whom are "graduating" each year out of Teach for America. Education spending represents 10 percent of GDP, second only to health care. There are 55 million students enrolled in K-to-12 education and 20 million in higher education. There are over 130,000 schools across 10,000 school districts.[6] Even 1 percent penetration of such a huge market results in a venture that, in time, cannot help but reach $100 million in revenue.

This gets young minds racing. So entrepreneurs enthusiastically design a product to improve the current system. This is not the hard part. It's often said that, in education, you can design a better product on the back of a cocktail napkin. The hard part—and where 90 percent of education entrepreneurs stumble—is distribution.

Distribution is critical in most industries. Take publishing, for example. Over the years, I've had some really bad ideas for things I might write. Lowlights include:

- The great American postal novel. The rags-to-riches story of a mailman who becomes a junk mail baron.
- A tale of a party planning firm that strikes it big with "Star Alliance Lounge" themed weddings and bar mitzvahs. Guests love the dim lighting, the opportunity to watch CNN at low volume, and the ability to bring their luggage.
- A story about a man in a smoked salmon suit who builds a bagel empire.
- A book about school supply salesmen in the Old West. A heroic journey from colored paper, glue and alphabet charts to supplementary materials and curriculum. At the end, they're writing history.

I never had the gumption to sally forth with any of these projects because I knew it would be a waste of time. How often does a self-published author find success? Well, at least once, I concede.

The greatest publishing success story since Harry Potter is E.L James's *Fifty Shades of Grey*. E.L. James began her writing career by posting fan fiction on a site dedicated to the "Twilight" series. She then reimagined her stories with different characters—a 21-year-old female student who feels passionately drawn to Christian Grey, a dominant businessman—and posted them on her own site. In May 2011, a small Australian publisher put out *Fifty Shades of Grey* as an e-book and print-on-demand paperback. By early 2012, the e-book was being devoured by working moms in Manhattan. It was then that a publisher at Random House's Vintage imprint decided she had found the next big thing. She traveled to the UK to meet James and won the bidding war for the trilogy. Within days of signing, Random House produced and distributed trade paperbacks and e-books and launched a major marketing effort. Reader demand exploded. A global debate on the sexy subject matter ensued. Each week brought a new print run, sometimes of over 900,000 copies. Random House now has sold over 100 million copies, with the first movie releasing early 2015.

On the other hand, surveys of self-published authors find that 50 percent earn less than $500 from their works, and that the average (skewed heavily by the top earners) is under $10,000. While Random House gets a hand for *Fifty Shades,* it is the exception that proves the rule.

It's rare that a great product finds distribution. This is especially true in education. While the need for great new products is higher than in any other sector of the economy, selling products to either K-to-12 or colleges and universities is incredibly challenging.

I've served on the boards of companies with great products that provide tremendous benefits to students. The typical progression of an education business is some initial adoption in local markets via pre-existing relationships. But hits are rare and word-of-mouth distribution almost unheard of. Closings are invariably pushed out 6, 12 and 18 months as it becomes clear that educational institutions—and the many decision makers involved in any purchase—have considerations other than student outcomes. To have any hope, companies must build (or buy or lease) a sales force. So the products that succeed aren't always the best products. Often, they're the ones represented in each territory by the longest-tenured reps who know a superintendent and perhaps lose money to him at poker every so often.

Sadly and ironically, in education distribution brawn beats product brains. And they don't teach that in Teach for America training.

Distribution is also critical for education products marketed directly to consumers. Up until 2009, the public higher education companies grew fat feasting on leads from lead aggregators. But it's slim pickings today. As the online education market matures, the lead aggregator and pay-per-click markets are in decline as consumers become more focused on return-on-investment and cost. According to a 2012 report from Parthenon, the leading consultancy in higher education, 44 percent of prospective online students have already spoken with an enrollment advisor about a program. As Parthenon says: "The low hanging fruit has been picked."[7] Leads aren't being generated and converted as they once were.

In need of new proprietary channels, the public companies have invested tens of millions of dollars in branding and advertising in the hope that prospective students will seek them out by name and that overall enrollment will rebound. So far no one has turned the corner.

What's true of the for-profits is equally true of traditional institutions. In today's market, developing a new higher education program without a clear and convincing distribution plan is tantamount to self-publishing a book. Success is the exception rather than the rule.

What all private sector players—from the budding entrepreneur to the public company—need to do is to ensure programs are addressing clear social or economic needs. If an institution or program is doing this, proprietary distribution channels should follow.

Elite colleges and universities may continue to develop and offer degree programs willy-nilly, but for the other 95 percent, I'd say that if a program doesn't have an inherent proprietary and moderately defensible distribution channel or is able to effectively tap an existing, functioning distribution channel, it's probably not a program that addresses a real social or economic need, and therefore it should be restructured or reconsidered. In other words, if your programs require lead aggregators and branding as the primary source of student acquisition, you may be in the wrong business.

The good news is that higher education is starting to become a lot more creative about distribution. There should be fifty shades of distribution in higher education. Going forward, college and university leaders will need to find their own shade before putting product pen to paper.

ELEVEN

AMERICAN HUSTLE

"Don't put metal in the science oven."

—"Irving Rosenfeld," *American Hustle*

ONE OF THE BEST SCENES IN RECENT FILM HIS-
tory occurs midway through *American Hustle,* the acclaimed 2013 David O.
Russell film. Jennifer Lawrence is Rosalyn Rosenfeld, the scene-stealing,
fire-setting wife of the con-man protagonist Irving Rosenfeld (Christian
Bale), who is given a revolutionary new product: a microwave, or as she
calls it, "a science oven." She's told not to put metal in the science oven, but
in the "do whatever I want" spirit of 1979, she does it anyway.

    American Hustle is a riotous pastiche of 1970s clothing and hairstyles,
showcasing the talents of four actors at the top of their games (and all
nominated for Academy Awards). But the real numbskull of the story is not
Rosalyn, who winds up with a mustachioed mobster, days of flames apparently behind her, but rather Bradley Cooper who plays the overzealous but
well-permed FBI agent Richie DiMaso.

DiMaso is the only character who ends up alone and betrayed because *American Hustle* is ultimately a story of government overreach undermining sensible policy. In this case, the policy—the good result everyone wants to achieve—is to rebuild Atlantic City and restore economic prosperity. And the overreach is the sting operation led by the ambitious and unstable DiMaso that ends up sidelining the most vibrant, passionate and effective force for achieving that goal, and the only good guy in the movie, Camden mayor Carmine Polito.

It's a story we're familiar with in higher education. Not the leisure suits and elaborate comb-overs, but rather the part about the government tripping over itself.

With the Obama administration in its final stretch, it's a good time to reflect on its record in the light of *American Hustle*'s disco ball. Because unlike the characters in *American Hustle* who prepared "from the feet up," the Obama administration has undermined nearly all of its higher education priorities, a remarkable feat that brings to mind Ronald Reagan's famous dictum: "The nine most terrifying words in the English language are, 'I'm from the government and I'm here to help.'"

STATE AUTHORIZATION

"All the razzle-dazzle that he does? It's not good, it's not real. It's fake . . . Am I crazy? I don't think so."

—"Richie DiMaso," *American Hustle*

Despite strong campaign support from college-age students and recent graduates, President Obama entered office without much focus on higher education. The education focus was understandably K-to-12, but his team soon came up with a policy priority for higher education. In his first State of the Union, the president stated that "by 2020, America will once again have the highest proportion of college graduates in the world."[1]

From the outset, as the president did not propose tens of billions in federal funds to build new campuses, it was clear to college cognoscenti that the only way to come close to this laudable goal would be to leverage online delivery. So what happened? Thanks to the hustle of the Department of Education (ED) in the 2009–10 Notice of Proposed Rulemaking (NPRM) process, we got state authorization. Specifically, 34 C.F.R. § 600.9(c) (2011) set forth that in addition to meeting the requirements of their own state, online providers would have to meet the requirements of all states in which students reside.

The officials at the ED responsible for this new rule must have been in a Richie DiMaso–esque haze of regulatory ambition in order to miss the impact state authorization would have on online education, and thus the administration's top higher education priority.

Before this rule, states and online providers coexisted in mutual ignorance. States that required authorization for any institution enrolling a student from the state were not considering enforcement against online providers. And states without authorization requirements were not considering enacting them.

The new federal rule awoke a sleeping giant. Suddenly states with authorization requirements began enforcing them. And states without them moved to enact them. For example, Maryland's proposed rule requires that universities enrolling students in the state meet defined criteria for curriculum design, faculty resources, library resources, and market demand— scrutiny comparable to the accreditation process. New programs outside of the liberal arts and sciences require submission of Maryland government and private survey data. Nevada's proposed rule defines education levels for instructors, requires a submission of course work, and dictates that if the regular instructor is replaced, the substitute must possess the same quali-fications. In the name of consumer protection, states like Maryland and Nevada have enacted what are effectively protectionist rules—either to generate revenue from fees or to protect their own public universities from competition.

This blizzard of state regulatory activity means significantly more work, expense and uncertainty for traditional colleges and universities to deliver online programs. Thanks to state authorization, it's more complex and expensive for small colleges and universities to operate online programs that enroll students from outside their state. This blocks development of online programs of any scale, and there's less innovation and enrollment growth as a result.

Then there's the potential harm to America's next great export. Of the many factors contributing to the dominance of the American economy in the twentieth century, two are worth noting here. First, the nineteenth century consolidation of a large national market under one set of rules: by 1890, the most advanced economies—America, Germany, Great Brit-ain, France—all possessed a national market for a broad range of products and services with no significant restrictions on trade. Second, among these countries, the United States was the largest national market in terms of population, natural resources and gross domestic product (GDP). The re-sult was unparalleled innovation and economic growth.

America has a number of inherent advantages in the coming twenty-first century global market for online education: market size, English lan-guage and the dominance of America's elite institutions (54 of the top 100). In fact, outside of entertainment and the consumer Internet, it's hard to think of an industry in which America approaches this level of dominance. (Recall that at America's postwar height, it only represented 40 percent of the global economy.)

Moreover, America has a head start with more than 15 percent of students studying entirely online and is home to nearly all of the innovations in online learning. This wouldn't be surprising to University of Minnesota economist Jacob Schmookler, who pointed out in his seminal work, *Invention and Economic Growth,* "the amount of invention is governed by the extent of the market."[2]

There must be Schmookler acolytes leading the ED's K-to-12 policy, because recent initiatives are Hamiltonian in their ambition to smear federal glue over the jigsaw-puzzle of our K-to-12 system. Race to the Top has required states seeking additional funding to reform policies around federally defined priorities and align English and math curricula and assessments to the new Common Core State Standards. The Common Core has now been adopted to some extent by 45 states and for the first time America has something approximating a national market in K-to-12 education. If Schmookler were still with us, he'd be predicting an explosion of innovation from publishers and education technology companies who will invest in systems and products to serve 45 states at a time.

But Schmookler is apparently unknown to the architects of the ED's state authorization rule; state authorization effectively balkanizes what had been the world's largest, most innovative market for online education.

Although controversy has prompted ED to delay the effective date of the rule several times (the new date is July 1, 2015), the horse has left the barn; states have begun regulating online education. Moreover, adding insult to injury, the ED is considering requiring states to make their authorization more rigorous. Called active review, state rules would need to meet certain standards in order to be eligible for Title IV financial aid funds. (Some states are still grandfathering authorization based on accreditation or prior operation in the state.) Despite resistance from every corner of higher education, the ED has not yet abandoned the idea of active review.[3]

As a result, large resource-rich universities like the University of Southern California report that in order to offer their new online MA in Teaching in partnership with 2U (an online course provider), they have had to comply with "a slew of obscure and irrelevant provisions, such as needing to submit typewritten applications and specifying the fire rating of file cabinets in which student records were to be stored."[4] On the other end of the spectrum, given the time and expense of complying with new state authorization rules, Troy University, an Alabama public institution with one online degree program, is waiting to review the geographic composition of online cohorts before deciding to comply with authorization or reject students. If it is innovation we seek, we are heading in the wrong direction.

CREDIT-HOUR RULE

"I was just trying to help you. If I wanted to bother you, if I really wanted to bother you . . . this is what I'd do . . . [He messes with Irving's comb-over] How's that? You bothered now?"

—"Richie DiMaso," *American Hustle*

Imagine that the US government imposed a new health care regulation: Patients with certain symptoms must spend a minimum length of time in treatment in order to qualify for reimbursement via Medicare or Medicaid. Looking up from the bottom of a fiscal chasm—one created in large part by skyrocketing health care costs—such a rule would be unthinkable. Doctors and nurses would provide additional care for the sole purpose of meeting the federal requirement; costs would jump and productivity would tank. In education, the second largest sector of the economy behind health care, such a rule is not only thinkable—it's another hustle perpetrated by the ED during the Obama administration.

Although the cost of health care has risen in recent decades, we are getting some value for our money—outputs (e.g., life expectancy) have improved. But education has seen scant improvements in terms of outputs. A professor at the University of Chicago once told University Ventures: "I still teach the same way Socrates taught 2,400 years ago—only not nearly as well."

One way to stymie productivity is to mandate that an "input" remains fixed. Inputs matter less than outputs. Yet a 2011 rule issued by the ED stated that access to Title IV financial aid—the lifeblood of US higher education—requires adherence to a strict measure of educational inputs.

A bit of history: 100 years ago, the Carnegie Foundation launched the first effort to formulate a means of accounting for inputs in higher education. The formulation was simple: X contact hours of faculty-led instruction + Y hours of student work outside the classroom over Z weeks = N credit hours. The Carnegie Unit was born.

Today, the Carnegie Unit remains the backbone input in American higher education. In the 2011 rulemaking process, the Department of Education hinged the entire system on this one input. It did so in a "Dear Colleague" letter from Eduardo Ochoa, assistant secretary for postsecondary education. Ochoa stated that the ED would require institutions participating in Title IV financial aid programs to follow the original Carnegie credit-hour formulation, which is based on "minimum amount of student work . . . in accordance with commonly accepted practice in higher education."[5]

With this ruling, the ED has equated the amount of student time that must be directed to the learning process with access to Title IV. Any attempt to innovate and increase productivity could be met with dire consequences. If a faculty member developed a way to teach the same material in half the time, she could jeopardize her program and institution's eligibility for Title

IV. Returning to the health care analogy: Productivity improvement doesn't simply mean the doctor isn't paid—it means the hospital gets shut down.

The credit-hour rule has interrupted a nascent process in which accreditation agencies were moving toward outcomes-based metrics for evaluating institutional quality. NACIQI—the Department of Education's advisory committee on accreditation—and regional accreditation groups such as the Western Association of Schools and Colleges (WASC) are shifting from inputs to outcomes in evaluating institutional effectiveness. The largest regional accrediting organization, the Higher Learning Commission, an early adopter of outcomes assessment through its AQIP (Academic Quality Improvement Protocols), received a grant from the Lumina Foundation to support its beta review of Lumina's Degree Qualifications Profile, intended to provide a standardized set of learning outcomes that should be achieved by students graduating at the associate, baccalaureate and master's degree levels.

In time, market innovations will persuade the ED to repeal or clarify the credit-hour rule. The tragedy of the credit-hour rule is that for the next several years, these new productivity-enhancing models will remain outside traditional higher education rather than evolving within colleges and universities.

GAINFUL EMPLOYMENT

"Everybody thought 'aww, Richie DiMaso's gonna stay in the office.' I'm outside on the field. I got people working for me, my ideas. I'm running the show. I'm the quarterback and I'm not going to settle. Those people, those corrupt people, I'm going after them."

—*"Richie DiMaso,"* American Hustle

In the fall of 2011, as the Occupy Wall Street movement spilled onto college campuses and became Occupy Colleges, the administration changed its higher education priority quicker than metal ignites in a science oven. Suddenly, affordability replaced completion as their policy goal. Myriad initiatives ensued, including scorecards and proposed ratings.

But when it comes to making higher education more affordable, it makes little sense to focus only on two- and four-year degrees. Much better to look at the full constellation of higher education options, especially the most affordable: certificate programs. Certificates are the fastest growing higher education credential. In 2013, 1 million certificates were awarded—more than triple the number of 20 years ago. A report from the US Census Bureau showed that 19 million US adults have earned a certificate, including 6.4 million who have no other education beyond high school.[6] The expected income bump from certificates is 10 percent overall and 17 percent for those with nothing else beyond high school. As we move down the path toward unbundling, one would reasonably assume that shorter, less-expensive certificate programs will play a huge role in improving affordability.

But reason is not in Richie DiMaso's vocabulary, nor apparently in the vocabulary of the officials at the ED who engineered the proposed Gainful Employment regulations. The ED heralded the Gainful Employment (GE) rule as a landmark accomplishment in the effort to protect students from the predatory practices of for-profit higher education institutions. Reinterpreting a provision of the Higher Education Act that had been dormant for 46 years, the GE introduced a formula designed to de-authorize higher education programs that burden graduates with a debt load that cannot be serviced by expected earnings from employment. Attractively simple in concept, GE was anything but that in construction and application. What was a two-word formulation exploded into a 5,500-word regulation requiring 157 pages of explanatory context.

They ensured it covered not only for-profit institutions—at which tuition is higher than at the state-supported institutions that enroll 70 percent of students and are therefore worthy of additional scrutiny—but every institution offering certificate programs. And since community colleges and traditional universities deliver two-thirds of certificate programs, these institutions now find themselves in the ED's crosshairs, subject to a bevy of new reporting requirements and ED sanction. Although the rules were struck down by a Washington, DC, District Court judge in the spring of 2013, the ED is intent on passing new, more restrictive rules.

The for-profit institutions that would be impacted by new-and-improved GE rules are caught in a regulatory vise: If they lower tuition in order to reduce student debt burdens, their 90/10 ratios will worsen—a legacy regulation that prohibits for-profit institutions from receiving 90 percent of their revenue from Title IV sources. So the combination of the new regulation on top of the old regulation creates a double whammy for college affordability.

Thanks to the GE hustle, the average cost of higher education may well increase.

U.S.A. NEWS & WORLD REPORT

"You think you're on the top of the list? What if you're not? What if you're not on that list? What if you're not even on that list at all?"

—*"Richie DiMaso," American Hustle*

The ED's big idea for 2013 and 2014 was to rate colleges based on who's providing the best value, hoping to eventually link these ratings to the distribution of Title IV financial aid. As President Obama said at Henninger High School in Syracuse on his 2013 back to school tour: "We're going to use these ratings, we hope, by working with Congress to change how we allocate federal aid for colleges. We've got to stop subsidizing schools that are not getting good results, start rewarding schools that deliver for the students and deliver for America's future. That's our goal."

The big event of the same period was the ambitious federal online application process for health care exchanges under the Affordable Care Act.

The college ratings effort has a few things in common with the ineffective rollout of the Obamacare Web site. First, it's controversial. Second, it will require pulling data from other federal agencies, such as the IRS, social security and other sources, which creates complexity. Third, it launches the federal government into a brand new sphere.

But unlike the Obamacare Web site, which hadn't existed previously, there is no shortage of private companies and organizations in the college ratings business. By my count, there are 15 in the United States and 16 globally. They are all expert at extracting available data, grouping institutions into categories, determining how much weight to give each variable and creating a consumer product.

The ED doesn't have much of a track record here. In particular, determining which inputs and outputs are most relevant for different categories of institutions—research universities and community colleges will likely have different metrics—is an ambitious project unto itself. President Obama might have a better chance of convincing Congress to tie federal financial aid to ratings of one kind or another now, before the ED releases ratings that are certain to be controversial. (Imagine if the administration had developed the Web site first and then attempted to persuade Congress to pass Obamacare. We'd have NObamacare.)

Unfortunately, the difficulty of the task ahead has not been acknowledged by the ED, which has taken an approach in stark contrast to the humility we hope to begin to see from higher education leaders. In a meeting with college presidents in the fall of 2013, Jamienne Studley, deputy un-dersecretary at the ED, said that rating colleges was "like rating a blender."[7] Since then, there has been a groundswell of opposition to the effort. "Apply-ing a sledgehammer to the whole system isn't going to work," said Robert G. Templin Jr., the president of Northern Virginia Community College. "They think their vision of higher education is the only one."[8]

Opposition from higher education has now manifested itself in Con-gress. In June 2014, Representatives Bob Goodlatte, Republican of Vir-ginia, and Michael Capuano, Democrat of Massachusetts, introduced a resolution opposing the ratings as "reductionist" and warned that they would "mislead" prospective students. Tennessee Senator Lamar Alexan-der, the top Republican on the Senate Education Committee, had been thinking about ways to block the ED from developing ratings but initially didn't think it would be necessary: "I expect that the president's proposal for a college ratings system will flop on its own face. We haven't seen it yet and we probably won't ever see it, because it's impossible to do it the way they're planning to do it with 6,000 autonomous institutions of higher education across the country."[9] In mid-June 2014, Senator Alexander indi-cated he would propose an amendment to a major appropriations bill that would prohibit further spending on the ratings system. Alexander said, "I have a serious practical concern with the department's ability even to begin this effort."[10]

There is an important role that the ED and the federal government should be playing in all this. There are two distinct elements of the ratings effort:

1. Ascertaining which input and output data are relevant, accurate and attainable for measuring the performance of different categories of higher education institutions.

2. Establishing ratings for these categories based on this data.

By pushing past the data issues in a rush to ratings, the ED is conflating these two activities, urging critics to not let the perfect be the enemy of the good as far as data is concerned. "The data is always imperfect," Secretary of Education Arne Duncan was recently quoted as saying. "We will use the best data we have."[11] In the spirit of the lean startup, Secretary Duncan promises that the ED will update the ratings as better data become available.

Secretary Duncan has had to respond to questions about data because everyone in higher education knows we have a Crisis of Data. So rather than overzealously attempting to launch ratings in 2015, the ED should focus on getting better data for everyone, including the dozens of incumbent ratings systems. The Voluntary Institution Metrics Project has identified three key roadblocks that need to be overcome in the absence of a federal unit-record database: first, the burden of tracking down students to see if they've completed at other institutions; second, tracking graduates' income and employment status, which requires pulling information from unemployment insurance databases—something that's only currently possible in a few states; and third, for student learning, there simply isn't enough standardized testing done on college students to correlate assessment results to student performance.

If ED can facilitate the production of consistent data in these areas rather than rolling out its own ratings according to a political calendar, and then allow existing ratings providers to access the new data, we'll end up with exactly the useful, consumer-friendly and popular ratings that President Obama is after. At that point, the idea of linking federal financial aid to ratings will be wholly uncontroversial. Which would be a nice change for the ED.

CONFLICTED

Like Irving Rosenfeld—highly conflicted between his mistress and business partner (Amy Adams) and his crazy wife—the ED is conflicted in achieving the administration's stated goals for higher education.

For the 2013 fiscal year (ending September 30), the ED generated a profit of $41.3 billion on federal student loans. And if not for the interest rate reduction deal in the summer of 2013, profits would have been $8 billion higher. These profits comprised nearly half the ED's total spending—the biggest share in over 15 years. So student loans are subsidizing almost half of the ED's budget and reducing the department's total cost to taxpayers to the lowest level since 2001.

Aside from the fact that only two companies in the world made more money than the ED in 2012 (Exxon Mobil and Apple), student advocates naturally point to the $1.2 trillion in outstanding student loan debt, that 41 percent of current undergraduates are taking federal loans (up from 35 percent four years ago), and that one in seven borrowers are now going into default, and ask whether the government should be making a profit on the backs of college students. Instead of generating profits, the ED could be providing full Pell grants to an additional 7.3 million students. In particular, when the US government can currently borrow for ten years at 2.71 percent, why does it need to charge students a premium of 75 percent to 169 percent, i.e., 2.05 percent for Stafford loans, 3.6 percent for graduate loans and 4.6 percent for parent loans? As Elizabeth Warren, the new liberal lion of the Senate says: "With college costs exploding and students being crushed by more than a trillion dollars in debt, I believe we should invest in our students—not make obscene profits off them."[12]

The ED's response is that it's not generating a profit, and that the accounting is complicated. These profits are being calculated based on the federal Credit Reform Act of 1990, which subtracts inflows from outflows and doesn't fully capture the risks and collection costs for which a private lender would account. At the same time, the ED's bosses in the White House continue to embrace the current accounting as a deficit reduction mechanism. As Jason Delisle, director of the federal education budget project at the New America Foundation, says, "They have gone out of their way to defend it."[13]

Three issues arise from this—all distinct, all important. The first is political: Should the ED generate a profit from student loans? The second, operational: Will the ED actually generate real profits or will it fail to collect?

But it's a third issue—the natural conflict at play here—that merits attention. Because while the administration proceeds at full speed with this strategy, it should recognize that the natural consequence of speeding is a ticket.

Research shows that tickets aren't simply a function of speeding; they're also a function of fiscal health. In a 2009 paper in the journal *Law and Economics,* Gary Wagner of the University of Arkansas and Thomas Garrett from the Federal Reserve Bank of St. Louis found that a 10 percent decline in the growth rate for a county's revenue prompted a 6.4 percent increase in the growth rate of traffic tickets the following year. Apparently this is already conventional wisdom in some states. Garrett and Wagner cite various officials predicting an increase in ticketing following a revenue loss or a failed initiative to increase local taxes.[14] Moreover, three states already limit the amount of revenue a city or county can generate from traffic tickets. And California allows municipalities to keep only 20 percent of revenue from tickets; the rest goes to the state. Another study in the *Journal of Public Economics* made a confirmatory finding: When law enforcement agencies are permitted to retain assets seized from drug arrests, the fraction of drug arrests to total arrests increases substantially.[15]

So even if student loan profits are paper profits, there's no question that the administration has an interest in sustaining paper profits to reduce paper deficits. Which raises the question: Could this incentive have a perverse impact on federal education policy? For example, while the ED's official policy is to promote income-based repayment—three separate but similar plans (Income Contingent Repayment, Income Based Repayment and Pay as You Earn) that cap monthly payments relative to income—mass adoption of such plans would eliminate paper profits.

So when Jen Mishory, deputy director of Young Invincibles, a not-for-profit organization representing 18-to-34-year-olds, testified that her organization recently held roundtables with students, and "none of the students we talked to had ever heard of Income Based Repayment," it may only be a coincidence. But Secretary Duncan himself has acknowledged that the ED hasn't "done the best job of getting the word out."

"It's just hard for me to control my passion. I'm a very passionate person."

—*"Richie DiMaso," American Hustle*

At the end of *American Hustle,* Richie DiMaso is let go by the FBI and receives no credit for the sting operation. Reason prevails. He would have benefited from reading the sign I taped to my door in college, taken from the serving line in the dining hall: "If you want less, tell me."

My roommates understood I wasn't talking about portion size, but rather a shared tendency to overdo things. My roommate Chris C. developed what he called "keg theory." Keg theory went like this: If we're going to have a few beers, we might as well get a case. And if we're going to get a case, we might as well get a pony keg. And if we're going to go through the trouble of getting a pony keg, we might as well get a keg. Needless to say, this slippery slope logic tended to have a negative impact on our health.

So did the pranks we would pull on each other. Chris crawled out on a steep roof just to lob pats of butter onto my skylight. The greasy smears never entirely disappeared. He also climbed through my skylight while I was out playing hockey, unlocked my door and removed all my furniture (then locked the door and exited back through the skylight). My roommate Dave took retribution for my putting grains of rice in his bed by setting my "If you want less, tell me" sign on fire. Looking back, it's amazing we survived.

It's equally amazing the ED has survived its own missteps that have directly undermined perfectly good policy goals. But it may be that someone has posted the "If you want less, tell me" sign on Secretary Duncan's door. Because the newest higher education priority (number 3 in five years) makes a lot of sense: increasing enrollment of low-income students at top colleges. This was the subject of a day-long meeting at the White House in February 2014 involving over 100 college and university presidents. The ED is absolutely right to focus the power of the bully pulpit on this issue, because low enrollment by low-income students at top colleges is a direct result of the financial aid policy that preceded the Obama administration: Families that earn $100,000 or more annually receive an average of $10,200 in federal financial aid while families that earn less than $20,000 annually receive an average of $8,000. "Undermatching"—where students from lower income families only apply to lower-tier, less expensive institutions— is one reason for this distortion.

So give the administration some credit for recognizing this issue and shining a spotlight on it. It demonstrates a level of reason that throws into stark relief the higher education policy hustle of the president's first term and gives us hope that the administration will figure out a way to rein in the Richie DiMasos who hustled state authorization and the credit-hour rule into law, and who continue to pursue Gainful Employment and federal college rankings.

THE UNIVERSITY IS (NOT YET) FLAT

What more could the administration do? How about taking a lesson from one of the twin quasars of the *New York Times* opinion page? In his 2005 book *The World Is Flat,* Tom Friedman illuminated the new digital face of globalization, its results and discontents. Friedman's "flat-world platform" permits individuals and small groups to compete globally, which results in massive increases in productivity and corresponding dislocations.

As Friedman wrote,

> We often forget that the software industry started out like a bad fire department. Imagine a city where every neighborhood had a different interface for connecting the fire hose to the hydrant. Everything was fine as long as your neighborhood's fire department could handle your fire. But when a fire became too big and the fire engines from the next neighborhood had to be called in, they were useless because they could not connect their hoses to your hydrants.

A key point of *The World Is Flat* is that this flattening occurred because of the alphabet soup of standards that the technology industry came to agree on in the 1980s and 1990s. According to Craig Mundie, Microsoft's chief research and strategy officer, TCP/IP, SMTP and HTML/XML "allowed people to exchange things other than standardized Word documents or e-mail. They enabled anyone to describe any kind of document they wanted—from an Amazon.com page to a credit card payment format—and transport it from machine to machine, and put it in front of your face, without any prior understanding or preparation between the person sending it and you, the person receiving it."[16] Friedman correctly reports that these standards beget other standards ("standards on top of standards"), like PayPal and Salesforce (and now Facebook and Twitter).

Regarding the current state of standards in higher education, most new attempts to develop learning experiences outside of the accredited university end up at the doorstep of the American Council on Education. ACE's Credit Course Review service determines "if the content, scope and rigor of the course . . . is equivalent to a college-level course."[17]

So instead of focusing on whether students are actually learning, would-be disrupters must attempt to retrofit learning experiences to a system of credit hours that was developed a century ago. It's tantamount to Sir Tim Berners-Lee consulting with the Union Pacific Railroad to determine the rules of the road for the Web.

The reason the university is not close to flat is the awful state of standards in higher education. First, as we've discussed, there is no agreement as to what student learning outcomes should be and how they should be measured. Second, there is no progress in defining the set of skills and knowledge that students should have upon completion of a given program of study. All this contributes to confusion around accreditation. What does it mean to be an accredited institution? What does a course credit actually mean? Based on some recent decisions by accrediting organizations, it seems like higher education is still in the railroad era and using different gauges of track in each region.

Information technology has coalesced around standards more easily than higher education has for two reasons. First, IT is an industry in which firms have a common incentive to maximize profits. In contrast, colleges and universities have complex decision sets that make intra-institutional consensus, let alone agreement, a challenge. Second, by setting standards, the IT industry believed it was establishing ground rules that would produce not only growth, but greater influence over the rest of the economy. In contrast, traditional universities take a more conservative approach: If we were to agree on a clear framework for credits and competencies, would it put us out of business in a decade?

The ED could do a great deal to establish a framework for credits and competencies. In the absence of federal action, this work is being led by the duo of Steve Klinsky, founder of the private equity fund New Mountain Capital, and Dave Bergeron, the ED's former acting assistant secretary for postsecondary education, now at the Center for American Progress. Klinsky and Bergeron are proposing to establish a "Modern States Accrediting Agency," an organization that would accredit courses rather than institutions and make the credits transferable to the existing system.[18] With course-level accreation, says Bergeron, "students might take their core lectures tuition-free and online from a nationally renowned professor in a MOOC and then attend supplementary weekly study groups with a live professor and other students in their hometowns, all at a lower overall cost than a traditional course today."[19]

It's not enough to keep Richie DiMaso at bay. There's no reason an individual of Bergeron's acumen and experience should have to leave the ED for such a worthy pursuit. The ED should be doing this itself. Failing to do so is tantamount to putting metal in the science oven.

TWELVE

HUMBLING
UNBUNDLING

I RECENTLY ATTENDED MY TWENTIETH COLLEGE reunion at Yale. Disneyfication of the campus notwithstanding, five minutes back in that gothic parkland I felt completely at home with my former roommates and friends. There was a lot of news about kids and careers. But it seemed more important to retell stories we already knew. We reminded ourselves about blue beads and other misdeeds. Stories of the time my roommates broke into the secret society Skull and Bones. Stories of BookWorld.

We also made new memories at the reunion. Walking around campus with my former college and law school roommate Dave made me feel 20 years younger. We went to the august Sterling Memorial Library and took turns pushing each other on a strange wheeled reading desk.

We explored the Hall of Graduate Studies (HGS), found a pile of blue examination books and distributed them to classmates we passed in the street, telling them to study because the final exam for the reunion was scheduled for Sunday at 9 a.m. in HGS 401.

When we left New Haven later that day, I'd like to think we left that college disrupted.

The Great Unbundling of higher education is underway. Within a few years we'll see the advent of double-click degrees and the rise of competency management platforms. The crises of today, of affordability, governance and data, will seem like the good old days—like record labels laughing about the "stress" they felt over the decline of the 8-track tape market.

In the long run, bundling in higher education will only continue where the bundle creates clear value or return on investment for students relative to unbundled alternatives. Other than at elite institutions, degrees are at risk of going the way of debutantes.

We are heading for a two-tier system of higher education. The bundled elite and unbundled for everyone else. Although appalling at first blush, it will be a more honest system than the one we have today where students at non-elite institutions are led to expect experiences and outcomes typical of elite colleges and then leave disappointed, indebted, and too often without the desired credential.

A two-tier system may prove to be the best outcome for institutions. Non-elite institutions will have no choice but to abandon isomorphism. It will be less drastic than what's currently happening in China, where the government has decided to convert at least half of its public universities to polytechnics in order to "reduce the huge number of university graduates with similar academic degrees competing with each other for the same jobs."[1] But it will get us to the same place in our own plodding, democratic way. It will also solve the "not invented here" syndrome. Intense budget-ary and accountability pressure on universities will require the humility to outsource, benchmark and adapt rather than invent.

A two-tier system may also prove the best outcome for students. In unbundling parlance, if many consumers no longer have the discretionary income to spend on cable—Time Warner and Comcast cable had 1.2 mil-lion customers unplug last year—they won't have the funds (or willingness to assume debt) to buy the higher education bundle. They would prefer to spend less for a value proposition best tailored to their own circumstances.

The organizers of our twentieth reunion thought it would be a good idea to arrange TED talks from a select group of classmates. If you're not familiar with TED talks, they are to education as McDonald's is to food: quick, cheap and bereft of nutrition (5–10 minute bursts of intellectual-sounding sound bites). One of the talks was from a classmate who founded a $100 million cloud-based software company. The effect of the reunion TED talks, I felt, was to divide our class into a small group of elites and the hoi polloi who didn't have much to say about the stress of an IPO.

Dave took matters into his own hands. Throughout the reunion, he would approach groups of classmates with the following shtick:

> Were you able to attend my TED talk? No? Let me tell you what it was about. I'm currently consulting for Disney. The goal is to rein-vigorate Epcot Center with Walt Disney's original vision . . . Did you know that Walt conceived of Epcot as a residential community? That's right, with people living there throughout the year. Say, how much do you spend on a typical vacation? $3,000 or $4,000? Did you know that for that amount, you could have a condominium for

a week each year at Epcot? In fact, I'm offering every member of the Yale Class of '94 vouchers on Delta to fly down and visit the development. Just think about it . . .

By turning reunion TED talks into a timeshare sales pitch, Dave burst the elitist bubble. It occurred to me that the Great Unbundling will do the same to elite universities. And because online and hybrid programs will make competencies visible to employers through double-click degrees and electronic portfolios, expect to see a new digital divide. The new digital divide will segment higher education providers into jobs-focused and employer-friendly institutions (i.e., online-plus-hybrid) and traditional campus-based institutions. It will accelerate the adoption of online learning and result in online taking additional market share from campuses for both adult learners and traditional age students.

It won't be long before the new digital divide humbles elite institutions by forcing them to adjust to double-click degrees and electronic portfolios if they want their graduates to remain competitive for entry-level jobs at the most desirable employers. Elite institutions will still provide a high-end version of a hybrid education and will continue to provide a rich, immersive extracurricular environment that can't be replicated digitally, but the outcome gap between elite and non-elite institutions will shrink. Employers will eventually view degrees similar to how we now view debutantes (i.e., a curiosity). In time, this will shrink the economic, racial and ethnicity gap between non-elite and elite institutions.

Despite the great fun I had in college and at the reunion, I can't help but think that these changes will be a very good thing for America, as well as for kids from foreign countries looking for an education so they can avoid a life of busing tables in restaurants.

I owe everything to my college experience. I met my wife, Yahlin, the very first day of class freshman year. She sat beside me in English 129 after I walked in the door with three different translations of Homer's *Iliad*. She was quoted in our wedding announcement as saying, "He was enough of a geek to walk in with three translations. And I was enough of a geek to be impressed by it." Now we have been together 21 years and have three beautiful and seemingly promising boys, Leo, Hal and Zev.

I feel I owe little to the college itself. I came to Yale reasonably literate and motivated and left four years later much the same (except four years older). As you can tell from my stories, very little of what I carry with me 20 years later is a result of the tuition I paid and the 120 credits I earned. What stuck were the interactions with classmates who also paid tuition for 120 credits. And my second go-round at Yale was pretty much a bust. (Did you know Yale Law School accepts bribes in return for JD degrees?)

Still, I was incredibly lucky. And I know now that the vast majority of tuition-paying students are not as lucky—at both non-elite and elite institutions. We can no longer afford for higher education to be a slot machine with a few hitting the jackpot and most going home with less money in their pockets and no better off.

The Great Unbundling will change higher education for everyone. And while it will be disruptive to the 25 million Americans engaged in this great enterprise, I'm confident we'll come out the other side much better off as a system and nation. The stories will be different—perhaps less amusing. But that's OK. We'll find amusement elsewhere. Higher education is serious business.

NOTES

CHAPTER 1

1. Bill Keller, "The university of wherever," *New York Times,* Oct. 2, 2011, http://www.nytimes.com/2011/10/03/opinion/the-university-of-wherever .html?pagewanted=all&_r=0 (accessed Feb. 4, 2014).

2. Jeffrey Selingo, *College Unbound: The future of higher education and what it means for students* (New York: Houghton Mifflin Harcourt, 2013), 4.

3. Paul Fain, "Within striking distance," *Inside Higher Ed,* July 29, 2014, https:// www.insidehighered.com/news/2014/07/29/clearinghouse-report-identifies -31-million-who-attended-college-didnt-complete (accessed Aug. 31, 2014).

4. "Non-traditional Undergraduates: Trends in Enrollment from 1986 to 1992 and Persistence and Attainment among 1989–90 Beginning Postsecondary Students, Statistical Analysis Report," Nov. 1996, National Center for Education Statistics Data Series: NPSAS: 87/90/93, BPS:90/94.

5. Arthur Levine, *Higher Learning in America: 1980–2000* (Baltimore: Johns Hopkins Univ. Press, 1994), xiii.

6. Ry Rivard, "Rankings noise," *Inside Higher Ed,* June 3, 2014, http://www.in sidehighered.com/news/2014/06/03/what-would-it-really-take-be-us-news-top -20#sthash.4oC45Vu3.lteMQpa5.dpbs (accessed June 13, 2014).

7. "The struggle to make the grade," *Economist,* Oct. 8–14, 2011, http://www .economist.com/node/21531468 (accessed Feb. 6, 2014).

8. R.R. Reno, "Teachers without students," *First Things,* June 2011, http://www .firstthings.com/web-exclusives/2011/06/teachers-without-students (accessed Feb. 6, 2014).

9. Paul Baskin, "AAU is accused of glorifying a limited view of higher education," *Chronicle of Higher Education,* June 3, 2014, http://chronicle.com/article/AAU-Is -Accused-of-Glorifying-a/146897/?cid=at&utm_source=at&utm_medium=en (accessed June 13, 2014).

10. Anthony P. Carnevale, Stephen Rose and Ban Cheah, "The College Payoff: Education, occupations, lifetime earnings," Aug. 5, 2011, Georgetown University Center on Education and the Workforce, http://cew.georgetown.edu/college payoff/ (accessed Feb. 6, 2014).

11. Anthony P. Carnevale, Nicole Smith and Jeff Cole, "Recovery: Job growth and education requirements through 2020," June 2013, Georgetown University Center on Education and the Workforce, http://cew.georgetown.edu/recovery2020/ (accessed Feb. 6, 2014).

12. Daniel de Vise, "U.S. falls in global ranking of young adults who finish college," *Washington Post,* Sept. 11, 2011, http://www.washingtonpost.com/local /education/us-falls-in-global-ranking-of-young-adults-who-finish-college /2011/08/22/gIQAAsU3OK_story.html (accessed Feb. 6, 2014).

13. Paul E. Lingenfelter, "Education Commission of the States," Dec. 8, 2011, http:// www.ecs.org/html/meetingsEvents/SC2011/paul.pdf (accessed Feb. 6, 2014).

14. President Barack Obama, "Address to Joint Session of Congress," Feb. 24, 2009, http://www.whitehouse.gov/the_press_office/Remarks-of-President-Barack -Obama-Address-to-Joint-Session-of-Congress (accessed June 18, 2014).

15. Samantha Grossman, "And the world's most educated country is . . ." *Time,* Sept. 27, 2012, http://newsfeed.time.com/2012/09/27/and-the-worlds-most -educated-country-is/ (accessed June 16, 2014).

16. "Educating Our Way to a Better Future," 2012, Video recording, http://www .edudemic.com/education-future-video/.

17. Pew Research Center, "Is college worth it?" *Daily Number,* June 2, 2011, http://www.pewresearch.org/daily-number/is-college-worth-it/ (accessed June 2, 2014).

CHAPTER 2

1. Scott Carlson, Goldie Blumenstyk and Andy Thomason, "Enrollment: A moving target for many institutions," *Chronicle of Higher Education,* Oct. 15, 2013, http://chronicle.com/article/Cloud-of-Uncertainty-Unsettles/142283/(accessed Mar. 31, 2014).

2. Douglas Belkin, "U.S. private colleges face enrollment decline," *Wall Street Journal,* Nov. 11, 2013, http://online.wsj.com/news/articles/SB1000142405270230 46724045791861531750945892 (accessed Mar. 31, 2014).

3. Associated Press, "Survey: Cost a growing factor in college decisions," *Journal,* Mar. 6, 2014, http://www.journal-news.net/page/content.detail/id/469327/Sur vey—Cost-a-growing-factor-in-college-decisions.html?isap=1&nav=5012 (accessed Mar, 31, 2014).

4. Bureau of Labor Statistics, reported in *New York Times,* "Fewer U.S. graduates opt for college after high school," Apr. 26, 2014.

5. Matthew Reed and Debbie Cochrane, "Student debt and the class of 2012," *Project on Student Debt,* Dec. 2013, Institute for College Access and Success, http:// projectonstudentdebt.org/files/pub/classof2012.pdf (accessed Mar. 31, 2014).

6. Bill Hardekopf, "More than half of student loans are now in deferral or delinquent," *Forbes,* Feb. 1, 2013, http://www.forbes.com/sites/moneybuilder/2013/02/01 /alarming-number-of-student-loans-are-delinquent/ (accessed Mar. 31, 2014).

7. Svati Kirsten Narula, "The myth of working your way through college," *Atlantic,* Apr. 1, 2014, http://www.theatlantic.com/education/archive/2014/04/the -myth-of-working-your-way-through-college/359735/ (accessed Apr. 2, 2014).

8. Dan Primack, "Occupation: From Wall Street to the university," *Fortune,* Oct. 5, 2011, http://finance.fortune.cnn.com/2011/10/05/occupation-from-wall-street-to-the-university/ (accessed Apr. 1, 2014).

9. Thomas G. Mortenson, "State funding: A race to the bottom," *American Council on Education,* Winter 2012, http://www.acenet.edu/the-presidency/columns-and-features/Pages/state-funding-a-race-to-the-bottom.aspx (accessed Apr. 1, 2014).

10. Grace-Marie Turner and Avik Roy, "Why states should not expand Medicaid,'" *Galen Institute,* May 1, 2013, http://www.galen.org/topics/why-states-should-not-expand-medicaid/ (accessed June 13, 2014).

11. Ben Wolfgang, "Colleges raise tuition as much as 22%," *Washington Times,* July 20, 2011, http://www.washingtontimes.com/news/2011/jul/20/state-cuts-push-colleges-to-hike-tuitions/ (accessed Apr. 1, 2014).

12. Karin Fischer and Jack Stripling, "An era of neglect," *Chronicle of Higher Education,* Mar. 3, 2014, http://chronicle.com/article/An-Era-of-Neglect/145045/ (accessed Apr. 1, 2014).

13. Ry Rivard, "State higher ed budgets rebound," *Inside Higher Ed,* Jan. 20, 2014, http://www.insidehighered.com/news/2014/01/20/state-higher-ed-funding-rebounds-not-yet-where-it-was-recession#ixzz2rYuyu74w] (accessed Apr. 1, 2014).

14. Timothy F. Slaper and Amia K. Foston, "Onward and upward with the cost of college," *Indiana Business Review,* Summer 2013, http://www.ibrc.indiana.edu/ibr/2013/summer/article1.html (accessed Apr. 1, 2014).

15. Mary Beth Marklein, "Colleges boost student fees to fill gaps in state funding," *USA Today,* July 27, 2011, http://www.ibhe.state.il.us/newsdigest/newsweekly/072811.pdf (accessed Apr. 2, 2014).

16. Georgia Tech Fact Book, "Tuition and Fees: Table 6.1, 6.2, 6.3," http://factbook.gatech.edu/student-related-information/tuition-and-fees-tables-6-1-6-2-6-3/ (accessed June 13, 2014).

17. Parimal M. Rohit, "Santa Monica College not included in two-tier tuition plan—for now," *Santa Monica Mirror,* Oct. 18, 2013, http://www.smmirror.com/articles/News/Santa-Monica-College-Not-Included-In-Two-Tier-Tuition-Plan—For-Now/38650 (accessed Apr. 2, 2014).

18. Ry Rivard, "Stopping a short-cut to in-state tuition," *Inside Higher Ed,* Apr. 1, 2014, http://www.insidehighered.com/news/2014/04/01/u-colorado-flummoxes-companies-promising-state-tuition-out-state-students (accessed Apr. 2, 2014).

19. Beckie Supiano, "Tuition increases slow down, but there's more to college affordability," *Chronicle of Higher Education,* Oct. 23, 2013, http://chronicle.com/article/Tuition-Increases-Slow-Down/142547/ (accessed Apr. 2, 2014).

20. Jeffrey Selingo, *College Unbound: The future of higher education and what it means for students* (New York: Houghton Mifflin Harcourt, 2013), 29.

21. Mark Kantrowitz, "Should more college financial aid be based on need, not merit?" *Wall Street Journal,* June 24, 2012, http://online.wsj.com/news/articles/SB10001424052970203370604577265350407194184 (accessed Sept. 8, 2014).

22. Ibid.

23. Christian Buss, Jeffrey Parker and John Rivenburg, "Cost, quality and enrollment demand at liberal arts colleges," *Economics of Education Review* 23 (2004):

65, http://labor.bnu.edu.cn/resource/jee/0402/Cost,%20quality.pdf (accessed Apr. 2, 2014).

24. Jerry Sheehan Davis, "Unintended consequences of tuition discounting," Lumina Foundation for Education 5, no. 1 (May 2013): 25. http://www.lumina foundation.org/publications/Tuitiondiscounting.pdf (accessed Apr. 2, 2014).

25. Donna Krache, "College cuts its tuition by 33%," *CNN Schools of Thought Blog,* Nov. 30, 2012, http://schoolsofthought.blogs.cnn.com/2012/11/30/college-cuts -its-tuition-by-33/ (accessed June 16, 2014).

26. Brad Tuttle, "One college slashes tuition by 22%, promises no more silly financial aid games," *Time,* Feb. 7, 2012, http://business.time.com/2012/02/07 /one-college-slashes-tuition-by-22-promises-no-more-silly-financial-aid-games/ (accessed June 16, 2014).

27. "Time is the enemy," Complete College America, Sept. 2011, http://complete college.org/docs/Time_Is_the_Enemy.pdf (accessed Apr. 3, 2014), 165.

28. Michael Stratford, "Best path for transfer credit," *Inside Higher Ed,* Aug. 20, 2014, https://www.insidehighered.com/news/2014/08/20/moving-community -college-four-year-university-most-likely-yield-succeful-credit (accessed Aug. 23, 2014).

29. Stephanie Owen and Isabel V. Sawhill, "Should everyone go to college?" Brookings Institution Research Papers, CCF briefs 50 of 51, May 8, 2013, http://www .brookings.edu/research/papers/2013/05/08-should-everyone-go-to-college-owen-sawhill (accessed Apr. 3, 2014).

30. Eric Risberg, "Half of new graduates are jobless or underemployed," *USA Today,* Apr. 23, 2012, http://usatoday30.usatoday.com/news/nation/story/2012-04-22 /college-grads-jobless/54473426/1 (accessed June 13, 2014).

31. Mary Beth Marklein, "Study: Nearly half are overqualified for their jobs," *USA Today,* Jan. 28, 2013, http://www.usatoday.com/story/news/nation/2013/01/27 /study-nearly-half-are-overqualified-for-jobs/1868817/ (accessed Sept. 8, 2014).

32. Hope Yen, "US wealth gap between young and old is widest ever," Associated Press, Nov. 7, 2011, http://news.yahoo.com/us-wealth-gap-between-young-old -widest-ever-050259922.html (accessed Sept. 8, 2014).

33. Richard Fry, D'Vera Cohen, Gretchen Livingston, Paul Taylor, "The rising age gap in economic well-being," *Pew Research Social and Demographic Trends,* Nov. 7, 2011, http://www.pewsocialtrends.org/2011/11/07/the-rising-age-gap-in-eco nomic-well-being/ (accessed June 13, 2014).

34. "The rising cost of not going to college," *Pew Research Social and Demographic Trends,* Feb. 11, 2014, http://www.pewsocialtrends.org/2014/02/11/the-rising -cost-of-not-going-to-college/ (accessed Apr. 3, 2014).

35. Dylan Matthews, "Tuition is too damn high Part II: Why college is still worth it," *Washington Post,* Aug. 27, 2013, http://www.washingtonpost.com/blogs /wonkblog/wp/2013/08/27/the-tuition-is-too-damn-high-part-ii-why-college-is -still-worth-it/ (accessed June 13, 2014).

36. Alan Benson, Raimundo Esteva, Frank S. Levy, "The Economics of B.A. Ambivalence: The case of California higher education," Sept. 13, 2013, http://ssrn .com/abstract=2325657 (accessed Apr. 3, 2014).

37. Hannah Seligson, "Job jugglers on the tightrope," *New York Times,* June 25, 2011, http://www.nytimes.com/2011/06/26/business/26work.html?adxnnl=1&p

agewanted=all&adxnnlx=1396536275-wXQdnpUpBtuFIS3anV9T8g (accessed Apr. 3, 2014).

38. Staci Zaretsky, "Law school applications plummet," *Above the Law,* Aug. 20, 2013, http://abovethelaw.com/2013/08/law-school-applications-continue-to-tumble/ (accessed June 16, 2014).

39. Joshua Wright, "The job market for lawyers: Side work on the rise amid continuing glut of new grads," *Forbes,* Jan. 10, 2014, http://www.forbes.com/sites/emsi/2014/01/10/the-job-market-for-lawyers-side-work-on-the-rise-amid-continuing-glut-of-new-grads/ (accessed Apr. 3, 2014).

CHAPTER 3

1. Jack Stripling, "Few trustees manage their president or push major changes, study finds," *Chronicle of Higher Education,* Dec. 14, 2011, http://chronicle.com/article/Few-Trustees-Challenge-Their/130099/?sid=at&utm_source=at&utm_medium=en (accessed May 5, 2014).

2. Ann Kirschner, "Innovations in higher education? Hah!," *Chronicle of Higher Education,* Apr. 8, 2012, http://chronicle.com/article/Innovations-in-Higher/131424/ (accessed May 5, 2014).

3. John Lachs, "Shared governance is a myth," *Chronicle of Higher Education,* Feb. 6, 2011, http://chronicle.com/article/Shared-Governance-Is-a-Myth/126245/ (accessed May 12, 2014).

4. Jeffrey Selingo, *College Unbound: The future of higher education and what it means for students* (New York: Houghton Mifflin Harcourt, 2013), 27.

5. Scott Carlson, "Administrator hiring drove 28% boom in higher ed workforce, report says," *Chronicle of Higher Education,* Feb. 5, 2014, http://chronicle.com/article/Administrator-Hiring-Drove-28-/144519/ (accessed May 5, 2014).

6. Glen Harlan Reynolds, "Degrees of value: Making college pay off," *Wall Street Journal,* Jan. 15, 2014, http://online.wsj.com/news/articles/SB10001424052702303870704579298302637802002 (accessed May 5, 2014).

7. Benjamin Ginsberg, *The Fall of the Faculty: The all-administrative university and why it matters* (New York: Oxford University Press, 2011).

8. Glen Harlan Reynolds, "Degrees of value: Making college pay off," *Wall Street Journal,* Jan. 15, 2014, http://online.wsj.com/news/articles/SB10001424052702303870704579298302637802002 (accessed May 5, 2014).

9. Tamar Lewin, "Student debt grows faster at universities with higher paid leaders, study finds," *New York Times,* May 19, 2014, http://www.nytimes.com/2014/05/19/education/study-links-growth-in-student-debt-to-pay-for-university-presidents.html?hp (accessed June 13, 2014).

10. Scott Carlson, "Administrator hiring drove 28% boom in higher ed workforce, report says," *Chronicle of Higher Education,* Feb. 5, 2014, http://chronicle.com/article/Administrator-Hiring-Drove-28-/144519/ (accessed May 5, 2014).

11. Ibid.

12. Courtney Rubin, "Making a Splash on Campus," *New York Times,* Sept. 19, 2014, http://www.nytimes.com/2014/09/21/fashion/college-recreation-now-includes-pool-parties-and-river-rides.html (accessed October 10, 2014).

13. Sara Guaglione, "University to spend record $220 million on construction," *Cavalier Daily*, Oct. 17, 2011, http://www.cavalierdaily.com/article/2011/10/university-to-spend-record-220-million-on-construction (accessed June 13, 2014).

14. Richard Vedder, "American higher education: An annual report card," *Chronicle of Higher Education*, Dec. 21, 2011, http://chronicle.com/blogs/innovations/american-higher-education-an-annual-report-card/31132 (accessed June 13, 2014).

15. Tamar Lewin, "Colleges increasing spending on sports faster than on academics, report finds," *New York Times*, Apr. 7, 2014, http://www.nytimes.com/2014/04/07/education/colleges-increasing-spending-on-sports-faster-than-on-academics-report-finds.html?_r=0 (accessed May 5, 2014).

16. Mark Bauerlein, "Professors on the production line, students on their own" (Future of American Education Project, Working Paper 2009-01, American Enterprise Institute), http://www.aei.org/files/1969/12/31/Bauerlein.pdf (accessed June 13, 2014).

17. James S. Fairweather, "Beyond the rhetoric: Trends in the relative value of teaching and research in faculty salaries," *Journal of Higher Education* 76(4), 2005, http://www.jstor.org/discover/10.2307/3838846?uid=3739448&uid=2&uid=3737720&uid=4&sid=21104300877473 (accessed June 13, 2014).

18. Richard Arum and Josipa Roksa, *Academically Adrift: Limited learning on college campuses* (Chicago: Univ. of Chicago Press, 2010), 35.

19. Ibid., 37; Philip Babcock, "Real costs of nominal grade inflation? New evidence from student course evaluations," Mar. 2009, Univ. of California-Santa Barbara, http://www.econ.ucsb.edu/papers/wp05-10.pdf (accessed May 12, 2014).

20. Selingo, *College Unbound*, 26.

21. Frank Bruni, "Class, cost and college," *New York Times*, Apr. 18, 2014, http://www.nytimes.com/2014/05/18/opinion/sunday/bruni-class-cost-and-college.html (accessed June 13, 2014).

22. Selingo, *College Unbound*, xv.

23. Bruni, "Class, cost and college."

24. Sean F. Reardon, "The widening academic achievement gap between rich and poor: New evidence and possible explanations," Center for Education Policy Analysis, Stanford University, http://cepa.stanford.edu/content/widening-academic-achievement-gap-between-rich-and-poor-new-evidence-and-possible (accessed May 5, 2014).

25. Jamie Merisotis, "Meeting the need for college graduates in Texas," Lumina Foundation Speech, Mar. 8, 2013, http://www.luminafoundation.org/about_us/president/speeches/2013-03-08.html (accessed May 7, 2014).

26. David Leonhardt, "The college dropout boom," *New York Times*, May 24, 2005, http://www.nytimes.com/2005/05/24/national/class/EDUCATION-FINAL.html?pagewanted=all&_r=0 (accessed May 7, 2014).

27. Danette Gerald and Kati Haycock, "Engines of inequality: Diminishing equality in the nation's premier universities," Lumina Foundation for Education, (Chicago: Education Trust, 2006), https://go8.edu.au/sites/default/files/events/geraldandhaycock_engines_of_inequality_diminishing_equity_in_the_nations_premier_universities_us.pdf (accessed May 7, 2014).

28. Amaal Abdul-Alim, "Expert: Stratification undermines American higher education's capacity for enabling social mobility," *Diverse: Issues in Higher Education*, July 24, 2012, http://diverseeducation.com/article/17239/ (accessed June 13, 2014).

29. Jason DeParlay, "Harder for Americans to rise from lower rungs," *New York Times*, Jan. 4, 2012, http://www.nytimes.com/2012/01/05/us/harder-for-americans-to-rise-from-lower-rungs.html?pagewanted=all (accessed May 7, 2014).

30. Ross Douthat, "College: The great unequalizer," *New York Times*, May 3, 2014, http://www.nytimes.com/2014/05/04/opinion/sunday/douthat-college-the-great-unequalizer.html (accessed May 7, 2014).

CHAPTER 4

1. Michael Lewis, Moneyball (New York, NY: W.W. Norton & Co., 2004), 16.

2. Advisory Committee on Student Financial Assistance, *Pathways to Success: Integrating learning with life and work to increase national college completion*, Feb. 2012, http://www2.ed.gov/about/bdscomm/list/acsfa/ptsreport2.pdf (accessed June 11, 2014).

3. Tamar Lewin, "College graduation rates are stagnant even as enrollment rises, a study finds," *New York Times*, Sept. 27, 2011, http://www.nytimes.com/2011/09/27/education/27remediation.html (accessed June 18, 2014).

4. Teresa A. Sullivan, Christopher Mackie, William F. Massy, and Esha Sinha, eds., National Research Council, *Improving Measurement of Productivity in Higher Education* (Washington, DC: National Academies Press, 2012), http://www.nap.edu/catalog.php?record_id=13417#description (accessed May 21, 2014).

5. "Brown M&Ms," 2012, Video recording, http://vimeo.com/36615187 (accessed June 11, 2014).

6. Ibid.

7. National Center for Education Statistics, *Digest of Education Statistics*, "Table 421. Federal on-budget funds for education by level/education purpose, agency and program, for selected fiscal years 1970–2012," http://nces.ed.gov/programs/digest/d12/tables/dt12_421.asp (accessed June 13, 2014).

8. Research! America, "2010 U.S. investment in health research," http://www.researchamerica.org/uploads/healthdollar10.pdf (accessed June 13, 2014).

9. Annie Murphy Paul, "The machines are taking over," *New York Times*, Sept. 14, 2012, http://www.nytimes.com/2012/09/16/magazine/how-computerized-tutors-are-learning-to-teach-humans.html?pagewanted=all&_r=0 (accessed May 23, 2014).

CHAPTER 5

1. Thomas L. Freidman, "Average Is Over," *New York Times*, Jan. 25, 2012, http://www.nytimes.com/2012/01/25/opinion/friedman-average-is-over.html?_r=0 (accessed September 2, 2014). David Brooks, "The Campus Tsunami," *New York Times*, May 4, 2012, http://www.nytimes.com/2012/05/04/opinion/brooks-the-campus-tsunami.html (accessed Sept. 2, 2014).

2. Jeremy Hsu, "Professor leaving Stanford for online education startup," *NBC news,* Jan. 25, 2012, http://www.nbcnews.com/id/46138856/ns/technology_and _science-innovation/t/professor-leaving-stanford-online-education-startup/#. VAXc0PldWd4 (accessed Sept. 2, 2014).

3. Jaques Steinberg and Edward Wyatt, "Boola, boola: E-commerce comes to the quad," *New York Times,* Feb. 13, 2000, http://www.nytimes.com/2000/02/13/week inreview/the-nation-boola-boola-e-commerce-comes-to-the-quad.html?page wanted=all&src=pm (accessed May 14, 2014).

4. Kevin Carey, "Stanford's credential problem," *Washington Monthly,* May 25, 2012, http://www.washingtonmonthly.com/college_guide/blog/stanfords_cred ential_problem.php (accessed Sept. 2, 2014).

5. Ibid.

6. Laura Pappano, "The year of the MOOC," *New York Times,* Nov. 2, 2012, http://www.nytimes.com/2012/11/04/education/edlife/massive-open-online -courses-are-multiplying-at-a-rapid-pace.html?pagewanted=all (accessed Sept. 2, 2014).

7. David F. Carr, "Udacity CEO says MOOC 'magic formula' emerging," *Information Week,* Aug. 19, 2013, http://www.informationweek.com/software/udacity -ceo-says-mooc-magic-formula-emerging/d/d-id/1111221 (accessed May 14, 2014).

8. Kris Hattori, "Governor Jerry Brown Udacity announce pilot program for $150 classes," *Edsurge,* Jan. 14, 2013, https://www.edsurge.com/n/2013-01-14-gover nor-jerry-brown-udacity-announce-pilot-program-for-150-classes (accessed Sept. 2, 2014).

9. Tamar Lewin, "California to give Web courses a big trial," *New York Times,* Jan. 15, 2013, http://www.nytimes.com/2013/01/15/technology/california-to-give -web-courses-a-big-trial.html (accessed June 18, 2014).

10. Carl Strumsheim, "Scaling back in San Jose," *Inside Higher Ed,* Dec. 18, 2013, http://www.insidehighered.com/news/2013/12/18/san-jose-state-u-resurrects -scaled-back-online-course-experiment-mooc-provider#ixzz30zFAkfJX (accessed May 20, 2014).

11. Gary Rivlin, "The tug of the newfangled slot machines," *New York Times,* May 9, 2004, http://www.nytimes.com/2004/05/09/magazine/09SLOTS.html?src =pm&pagewanted=8 (accessed Sept. 2, 2014).

12. Dirk Hanson, "Addiction machines: How slots are designed for compulsive play," *Addiction Inbox: The science of substance abuse,* Mar. 4, 2013, http://addiction -dirkh.blogspot.ca/2013/03/addiction-machines-how-slots-are.html (accessed May 20, 2014).

13. Karen Collins, "Addictive gameplay: What casual game designers can learn from slot machine research," *Acadamica.edu,* http://www.academia.edu/256033/_Ad dictive_Gameplay_What_Casual_Game_Designers_Can_Learn_from_Slot _Machine_Research (accessed May 20, 2014).

14. Amy J. Claxton, Joyce Cramer, Courtney Pierce, "A systematic review of the association between dose regimens and medication compliance," *Clinical Therapeutics* 23:8, 1296-1310, http://www.clinicaltherapeutics.com/article /S0149-2918(01)80109-0/abstract?showall=true=?showall=true (accessed June 2, 2014).

15. Eduardo Sabaté, ed., *Adherence to Long-term Therapies: Evidence for Action*, World Health Organization, 2003, http://www.who.int/chp/knowledge/publi cations/adherence_full_report.pdf.

16. Ellie Ashford, "New college students can drown in a sea of choices," *Community College Daily*, May 10, 2013, http://www.ccdaily.com/Pages/Campus-Issues /New-college-students-can-drown-in-a-sea-of-choices-.aspx (accessed June 2, 2014).

17. Bruce Vandal, "West Virginia throwing lifeline to students," *Complete College America*, May 30, 2014, http://completecollege.org/west-virginia-throwing-life line-to-students/ (accessed June 2, 2014).

18. Andy Reinhardt, "Steve Jobs: 'There's sanity returning,'" *Business Week*, May 25, 1998, http://www.businessweek.com/1998/21/b3579165.htm (accessed June 2, 2014).

19. Rebecca Merrett, "How gamification improved student learning at Kaplan University," *CIO*, June 6, 2014, http://www.cio.com.au/article/546969/how_gami fication_improved_student_engagement_kaplan_university/ (accessed June 13, 2014).

20. Matt Richtel, "In classrooms of the future, stagnant scores," *New York Times*, Sept. 3, 2011, http://www.nytimes.com/2011/09/04/technology/technology-in -schools-faces-questions-on-value.html?pagewanted=all (accessed May 20, 2014).

CHAPTER 6

1. National Center for Education Statistics, "Table 301.10 Enrollment, staff, and degrees/certificates conferred in degree-granting and non-degree-granting post-secondary institutions, by control and level of institution, sex of student, type of staff, and level of degree: Fall 2010, fall 2011, and 2011–12," *Digest of Education Statistics* http://nces.ed.gov/programs/digest/d13/tables/dt13_301.10.asp (accessed June 2, 2014).

2. Anant Agarwal, "Unbundled: Reimagining higher education," *Huffington Post*, Sept. 12, 2013, http://www.huffingtonpost.com/anant-agarwal/unbundled-re imagining-higher-education_b_4414048.html (accessed May 26, 2014).

3. Yannis Bakos and Erik Brynjolfsson, "Bundling information goods: Pricing, profits, and efficiency," *Management Science* 45:12, 1999: 1613–1630, http:// pubsonline.informs.org/doi/abs/10.1287/mnsc.45.12.1613 (accessed May 26, 2014).

4. Accenture, "Where the cloud meets reality: Scaling to succeed in new business models," 2012, http://www.accenture.com/SiteCollectionDocuments/PDF/Accen ture-Where-the-Cloud-Meets-Reality.pdf#zoom=50 (accessed May 26, 2014).

5. Mark Washburn, "Davidson college scrubbing historic perk for students," *Charlotte Observer*, May 7, 2014, http://www.charlotteobserver.com/2014/05/07/48 94167/davidson-college-scrubbing-historic.html#.U4Njl_ldWcE (accessed May 26, 2014).

6. Paul Fain, "Transcript for work," *Inside Higher Ed*, Feb. 12, 2013, https://www .insidehighered.com/news/2013/02/12/technical-college-puts-job-readiness -and-attendance-scores-transcripts (accessed Aug. 30, 2014).

7. Carl Straumsheim, "Promising portfolios," *Inside Higher Ed,* Jan. 27, 2014, http://www.insidehighered.com/news/2014/01/27/aacu-conference-shows-ple nty-uses-e-portfolios-also-pitfalls-hype#ixzz2rcSS1e00 (accessed May 26, 2014).
8. "Blackboard integrates MyEdu profile into Learn," *Inside Higher Ed,* June 2, 2014, http://www.insidehighered.com/quicktakes/2014/06/02/blackboard-inte grates-myedu-profiles-learn#sthash.gDeNaaLJ.dpbs (accessed June 13, 2014).

CHAPTER 7

1. Ann Kirschner, "Innovations in higher education? Hah!" *Chronicle of Higher Education,* Apr. 8, 2012, http://chronicle.com/article/Innovations-in-Higher /131424/ (accessed June 16, 2014).
2. Institute of Education Sciences, "CCD quick facts," National Center for Education Statistics, http://nces.ed.gov/ccd/quickfacts.asp (accessed June 16, 2014).
3. John W. Curtis, "Trends in instructional staff employment status, 1975–2011," AAUP Research Office, Apr. 2013, http://www.aaup.org/sites/default/files /files/AAUP_Report_InstrStaff-75-11_apr2013.pdf (accessed June 16, 2014).
4. Steve Kolowich, "The lecturers' filibuster," *Inside Higher Ed,* Oct. 11, 2011, http://www.insidehighered.com/news/2011/10/11/university_of_california _lecturers_union_says_it_can_block_online_programs#sthash.IPCdX7Z0 .dpbs (accessed June 16, 2014).
5. Andrew Rosenthal, "The trouble with online college," *New York Times,* Feb. 19, 2013, http://www.nytimes.com/2013/02/19/opinion/the-trouble-with-online-c ollege.html?_r=0 (accessed June 16, 2014).
6. Andrew Leonard, "Conservatives declare war on college," *Salon,* Feb. 22, 2013, http://www.salon.com/2013/02/22/conservatives_declare_war_on_college/ (accessed June 16, 2014).
7. Lance Murphy, "Profits and questions at online charter schools," *New York Times,* http://www.nytimes.com/2011/12/13/education/online-schools-score-b etter-on-wall-street-than-in-classrooms.html?pagewanted=all (accessed June 16, 2014).
8. John E. Hunter and Ronda F. Hunger, "Validity and utility of alternative predictors of job performance," *Psychological Bulletin* 96 (1984), 72–98.
9. *Uniform Guidelines on Employee Selection Procedures: A free resource for HR professionals,* Biddle Consluting Group, http://www.uniformguidelines.com/uniform guidelines.html (accessed June 16, 2014).
10. ACT, Research and Policy Reports, http://www.act.org/research-policy/research -reports/ (accessed June 16, 2014).
11. Peter Cappelli, *Why Good People Can't Get Good Jobs* (Philadelphia: Wharton Digital Press, 2012).
12. Kevin Carey, "A matter of degrees," *A Report by the Education Trust,* 2004, http:// planning.ucsc.edu/retention/Docs/a_matter_of_degrees.pdf (accessed May 29, 2014).
13. Doug Shapiro, Afet, Dundar, Mary Ziskin, Xin Yuan, and Ann Harrell, *Completing College: A State-Level View of Student Attainment Rates* (Signature Report No. 6a). (March 2014). Herndon, VA: National Student Clearinghouse Research

Center, http://nscresearchcenter.org/wp-content/uploads/NSC_Signature_Rep ort_6_StateSupp.pdf (accessed May 29, 2014).

14. Jean Johnson, Jon Rochkind, Amber N. Ott and Samantha DuPont, *With Their Whole Lives Ahead of Them,* Public Agenda, http://www.publicagenda.org/files /theirwholelivesaheadofthem.pdf (accessed May 29, 2014).

15. Zineta Kolenovic, Donna Linderman, Melinda Mechur Carp, "Improving student retention and graduation via comprehensive supports: Two and three year outcomes from CUNY's Accelerated Study in Associate Programs (ASAP)," https://www.cuny.edu/academics/programs/notable/asap/Pagesfrom2012Con ferenceProceedings.pdf (accessed September 2, 2014).

16. Caroline Porter, "Community-college freshmen get more direction," *Wall Street Journal,* Jan. 6, 2014, http://online.wsj.com/news/articles/SB100014240527023 03330204579248441748612968 (accessed May 29, 2014).

17. Seth Zweifler, "A new community college keeps students on track with structure," *Chronicle of Higher Education,* May 27, 2014, http://chronicle.com/article/A -New-Community-College-Keeps/146731/?cidA=cc&utm_source=cc&utm _medium=en (accessed May 29, 2014).

18. Originally aired Sunday, May 20, 2012, http://www.cbsnews.com/news/billion aire-offers-college-alternative/ (accessed Sept. 2, 2014).

19. Richard Levin, "Liberal education and the western tradition," *Yale Alumnai Magazine,* http://archives.yalealumnimagazine.com/issues/95_07/levin.html (accessed Sept. 2, 2014).

20. Richard Arum and Josipa Roksa, *Academically Adrift: Limited learning on college campuses* (Chicago: Univ. of Chicago Press, 2010).

21. Matthew Philips, "It's not a skills gap: U.S. workers are overqualified, undertrained," *Business Week,* Aug.14, 2014, http://www.businessweek.com/articles /2014-08-19/its-not-a-skills-gap-u-dot-s-dot-workers-are-overqualified-under trained (accessed Sept. 2, 2014).

22. Corporate Voice for Working Families, *A Talent Development Solution: Exploring business drivers and returns in learn and earn partnerships,* Sept. 2012, http:// www.cewd.org/Documents/LearnEarn_Report2_web.pdf (accessed May 29, 2014).

23. Jon Marcus "Putting college degrees to work," *Boston Globe Magazine,* Mar. 2, 2012, http://www.bostonglobe.com/magazine/2012/03/02/how-colleges-can -help-fix-issue-unfilled-job-openings-massachusetts/1uJpWtkVTXtYT9oLVxT QrJ/story.html (accessed June 16, 2014).

CHAPTER 8

1. Keith Bradshier, "In China, families bet it all on college for their children," *New York Times,* Feb. 16, 2013, http://www.nytimes.com/2013/02/17/business/in -china-families-bet-it-all-on-a-child-in-college.html?pagewanted=all&_r=0 (accessed June 2, 2014).

2. Center for World-Class Universities of Shanghai Jiao Tong University, "Academic ranking of world universities 2013," Shanghai Ranking Consultancy, http://www.shanghairanking.com/ARWU2013.html (accessed June 2, 2014).

3. Diana Farrell and Andrew Grant, *Addressing China's Looming Talent Shortage,* Report, McKinsey Global Institute, Oct. 2005, http://www.mckinsey.com/in sights/china/addressing_chinas_looming_talent_shortage (accessed June 2, 2014).

4. "Educators not surprised by exam cheating survey," *Thanh Nien news.com,* July 27, 2012, http://thanhniennews.com/society/educators-not-surprised-by-exam cheating-survey-5903.html (accessed June 5, 2014).

5. Michael J. Silverstein and Abheek Singhi, "Can U.S. universities stay on top?" *Wall Street Journal,* Sept. 28, 2012, http://online.wsj.com/news/articles/SB1000 08723963904443588045780185319278561700 (accessed June 2, 2014).

6. Cheng Yingqi, "University partnerships can be shaky," *China Daily,* Aug. 14, 2012, http://usa.chinadaily.com.cn/china/2012-08/14/content_15676280.htm (accessed June 2, 2014).

7. Silverstein and Singhi, "Can U.S. universities stay on top?"

8. Jeff Yang, "Are your kids smart enough for China's toughest test?" *Wall Street Journal,* June 26, 2012, http://blogs.wsj.com/speakeasy/2012/06/26/are-your -kids-smart-enough-for-chinas-toughest-test/ (accessed June 2, 2014).

9. Silverstein and Singhi, "Can U.S. universities stay on top?"

10. McKinsey China, "The $250 billion dollar question: Can China close the skills gap," Jun. 25, 2013 http://www.mckinseychina.com/the-250-billion-question -can-china-close-the-skills-gap/ (accessed Sept. 3, 2014).

   Andrew Winterbottom, "Improving rankings for Chinese universities," *China Outlook,* July 13, 2013, http://china-outlook.net/improving-rankings-for -chinese-universities/ (accessed June 2, 2014).

11. Mona Mourshed, Diana Farrell, Dominic Barton, "Education to employment: Designing a system that works," McKinsey Center for Government, http://mc kinseyonsociety.com/downloads/reports/Education/Education-to-Employment _FINAL.pdf (accessed June 3, 2014), 18.

12. Stephen Connelly and Alan Olsen, "Education as an export for Australia: Green shoots, first swallows, but not quite out of the woods yet," Australian International Education Conference, Oct. 10, 2013, http://www.spre.com.au/down load/AIEC2013ModelingPaper.pdf (accessed June 3, 2014).

13. Jerry Useem, "Business school, disrupted," *New York Times,* May 31, 2014, http://www.nytimes.com/2014/06/01/business/business-school-disrupted.html ?hp&_r=0 (accessed June 4, 2014).

14. Sam Webb, "The real-life Hogwarts! Chinese university building bears uncanny resemblance to the magical Harry Potter school," *Mail Online,* Apr. 29, 2014, http://www.dailymail.co.uk/news/article-2616043/The-real-life-Hogwarts -University-building-China-bears-uncanny-resemblance-magical-Harry-Potter -school.html (accessed June 4, 2014).

CHAPTER 9

1. Ann Kirschner, "Innovation in higher education? Hah!," *Chronicle Review,* Apr. 13, 2012, http://www.macaulay.cuny.edu/about/press/Innovation-in-Higher-Ed .pdf (accessed June 6, 2014).

2. John Lewis, "Keith Jarrett's Köln concert," *Guardian,* June 17, 2011, http://www .theguardian.com/music/2011/jun/17/keith-jarrett-koln-concert (accessed June 5, 2014).

3. John Fordham, "50 great moments in Jazz: Keith Jarrett," *Guardian,* Jan. 31, 2011, http://www.theguardian.com/music/musicblog/2011/jan/31/50-great-moments -jazz-keith-jarrett (accessed Sept. 3, 2014); Corinna Da Fonseca-Wollheim, "A jazz night to remember," *Wall Street Journal,* Oct. 11, 2008, http://online.wsj .com/news/articles/SB1223367103134923957 (accessed Sept. 3, 2014).

4. Jeff Selingo, Kevin Carey, Hilary Pennington, Rachel Fishman, and Iris Palmer, "The next generation university," *New America Foundation,* May 2013, http:// education.newamerica.net/sites/newamerica.net/files/policydocs/Next_Genera tion_University_FINAL_FOR_RELEASE.pdf (accessed June 6, 2014).

5. *Annual Research Report FY2012,* Arizona Board of Regents, https://azregents .asu.edu/ABOR%20Reports/2012-Annual-Research-Report.pdf (accessed June 6, 2014).

6. Sarah Auffret, "ASU now among top 3 research universities for Fulbright awards," *ASU News,* Oct. 30, 2013, 1, https://asunews.asu.edu/20131030-asu-ful brights (accessed June 6, 2014).

7. Michael M. Crow, "Reviving our economy: Supporting a 21st century workforce," *Testimony of Michael M. Crow, President, Arizona State University,* Hearing Before Committee on Education and the Workforce, Mar. 20, 2014, 14, http://edwork force.house.gov/uploadedfiles/crow_testimony_final.pdf (accessed June 6, 2014).

8. Ibid.

9. Ibid., 20.

10. Douglas Belkin, "Design for a new college, " *Wall Street Journal,* Mar. 9, 2014, http://online.wsj.com/news/articles/SB100014240527023046268045793632311 57886544 (accessed Sept. 3, 2014).

11. Jim Yardley, "A singing nun for a reality TV world," *New York Times,* May 6, 2014, http://www.nytimes.com/2014/05/07/world/europe/a-singing-nun-for-a -reality-tv-world.html?_r=0 (accessed June 6, 2014).

12. "University announces creation of online chapel," *Inside Higher Ed,* May 5, 2014, http://www.insidehighered.com/quicktakes/2014/05/05/university-announces -creation-online-chapel#sthas1zlllEs.pnN302n7.dpbs (accessed June 6, 2014).

CHAPTER 10

1. Paul Gladder and Peter Wonnacot, "Why private colleges are surging in India," *Wall Street Journal,* Mar. 29, 2007, http://online.wsj.com/news/articles /SB117511076960152221 (accessed June 9, 2014).

2. Dante J. Salto, "The for-profit higher education giant," *University World News,* Jan. 17, 2014, http://www.universityworldnews.com/article.php?story=2014011 5175750863 (accessed June 9, 2014).

3. Tristan McCowan, "The growth of higher education in Brazil: Implications for equity and quality," *Journal of Higher Education,* 19(4), 2004, 453–472, http:// www.academia.edu/234315/The_growth_of_private_higher_education_in _Brazil_implications_for_equity_and_quality (accessed June 9, 2014).

4. Sam Dillon, "New Jersey college is beset by accusations," *New York Times,* Dec. 21, 2009, http://www.nytimes.com/2009/12/22/education/22stevens.html?pa gewanted=all&_r=0 (June 9, 2014).

5. Daniel de Vise, "Eight scandals that ended college presidencies," *Washington Post,* Nov. 21, 2011, http://www.washingtonpost.com/blogs/college-inc/post /eight-scandals-that-ended-college-presidencies/2011/11/21/gIQA4diYiN_blog .html (accessed June 9, 2014).

6. The Center for Education Reform, "K-12 Facts," *Digest 2011,* http://www.ed reform.com/2012/04/k-12-facts/#enrollment (accessed June 9, 2014).

7. Chris Ross, "Where have all the students gone? Enrollment trends in private sector higher education," *Parthenon Perspectives,* Mar. 2012, http://www.par thenon.com/GetFile.aspx?u=%2FLists%2FThoughtLeadership%2FAttachmen ts%2F44%2FWhere%2520Have%2520the%2520Students%2520Gone_Final _March%25202012.pdf (accessed June 9, 2014).

CHAPTER II

1. Samantha Grossman, "And the world's most educated country is . . ." *Time,* Sept. 27, 2012, http://newsfeed.time.com/2012/09/27/and-the-worlds-most -educated-country-is/ (accessed June 16, 2012).

2. Jacob Schmookler, *Invention and economic growth* (Cambridge: Harvard University Press, 1966), 104.

3. Dan Bauman, "Online learning groups warn against federal action on 'state authorization'," *Chronicle of Higher Education,* June 14, 2014, http://chronicle .com/article/Online-Learning-Groups-Warn/147147/?cid=at&utm_source=at &utm_medium=en (accessed June 18, 2014).

4. Ben Wildavsky and Robert E. Liton, "It's time to go back to school on higher ed reform," *Huff Post College,* May 7, 2012, http://www.huffingtonpost.com /ben-wildavsky/higher-education-reform_b_1651914.html (accessed June 17, 2014).

5. Eduardo M. Ochoa, "DCL ID: Gen-11-06: Subject: Guidance to institutions and accrediting agencies regarding a credit hour as defined in the final regulations published on October 29, 2010," IFAP, Mar. 18, 2011, https://ifap.ed.gov /dpcletters/GEN1106.html (accessed June 17, 2014).

6. Stephanie Ewert and Robert Kominsky, "Measuring alternative education credentials: 2012," *Household Economic Studies,* Jan. 2014, http://www.census.gov /prod/2014pubs/p70-138.pdf (accessed June 17, 2014).

7. Michael D. Shear, "Colleges rattled as Obama presses rating system," *New York Times,* May 26, 2014, http://www.nytimes.com/2014/05/26/us/colleges -rattled-as-obama-presses-rating-system.html?src=me&_r=1#story-continues-3 (accessed June 16, 2014).

8. Ibid.

9. Michael Stratford, "Obama defends college ratings," *Inside Higher Ed,* June 6, 2011, http://www.insidehighered.com/news/2014/06/11/obama-defends-college-rat ings-system-amid-growing-backlash-capitol-hill#ixzz34KCdTuPS (accessed June 16, 2014).

10. "Top senate republican seeks to block college ratings," *Inside Higher Ed,* June 13, 2014, http://www.insidehighered.com/quicktakes/2014/06/13/top-senate-repu blican-seeks-to-block-college-ratings#ixzz34aeS84yy (accessed June 16, 2014).

11. Kelly Field, "Students, professors and administrators are wary of President Obama's plan to rate colleges," *Chronicle of Higher Education,* Nov. 15, 2013, http://chronicle.texterity.com/chronicle/20131115a?pg=8#pg8 (accessed June 17, 2014).

12. Shahien Nasiripour, "Federal student loan profits help Duncan cut education spending to lowest level since 2001," *Huffington Post,* Nov. 18, 2013, http://www .huffingtonpost.com/2013/11/18/federal-student-loan-profits_n_4283765.html (accessed June 17, 2014).

13. Ibid.

14. Thomas A Garrett and Gary A. Wagner, "Red Ink in the Rearview Mirror: Local Fiscal Conditions and the Issuance of Traffic Tickets," *Journal of Law and Economics* 52, no. 1 (Feb. 2009).

15. Katherine Baicker and Mireille Jacobson, "Finders Keepers: Forfeiture laws, policing incentives and local budgets," *Journal of Public Economics* 91 (2007): 2113–2136, http://users.nber.org/~jacobson/BaickerJacobson2007.pdf (accessed June 17, 2014).

16. Thomas L. Freidman, *The World Is Flat: A brief history of the twenty-first century* (New York: Farrar, Straus & Giroux, 2005), 82.

17. American Council on Education, "ACE Credit Course Review," http://www.ace net.edu/news-room/Pages/ACE-CREDIT-Course-Review.aspx (accessed June 17, 2014).

18. David Bergeron and Steven Klinsky, "Debt-free degrees," *Inside Higher Ed,* Oct. 28, 2013, http://www.insidehighered.com/views/2013/10/28/essay-need-new -innovation-focused-accreditor#sthash.dCADLjqY.wLRVdRGW.dpbs (accessed June 16, 2014).

19. Karen Weise, "Tea Partiers and liberals: Everyone hates the federal financial aid system," *Bloomberg BusinessWeek,* June 16, 2014. http://www.business week.com/articles/2014-06-16/tea-partiers-and-liberals-everyone-hates-the-fed eral-financial-aid-system

CHAPTER 12

1. Yojana Sharma, "Major reform as 600 universities become polytechnics," *University World News* (324) June 12, 2014, http://www.universityworldnews.com /article.php?story=20140612080509913 (accessed June 17, 2014).

INDEX

INDEX